Conversations with
Zygmunt Bauman

Conversations
with
Zygmunt Bauman

Zygmunt Bauman and Keith Tester

Polity

First published in 2001 by Polity Press
in association with Blackwell Publishers Ltd

Editorial office:
Polity Press
65 Bridge Street
Cambridge CB2 1UR, UK

Marketing and production:
Blackwell Publishers Ltd
108 Cowley Road
Oxford OX4 1JF, UK

Published in the USA by
Blackwell Publishers Inc.
350 Main Street
Malden, MA 02148, USA

ISBN 0-7456-2664-5
ISBN 0-7456-2665-3 (pbk)

A catalogue record for this book is available from the British Library and has been applied for from the Library of Congress.

Typeset in 11 on 13 pt Berling
by SetSystems Ltd, Saffron Walden, Essex
Printed in Great Britain by MPG Books Ltd, Bodmin, Cornwall

This book is printed on acid-free paper.

Contents

And Polo said: 'The inferno of the living is not something that will be: if there is one, it is what is already here, the inferno where we live every day, that we form by being together. There are two ways to escape suffering it. The first is easy for many: accept the inferno and become such a part of it that you can no longer see it. The second is risky and demands constant vigilance and apprehension: seek and learn to recognize who and what, in the midst of the inferno, are not inferno, then make them endure, give them space.'

Italo Calvino, *Invisible Cities*

Preface

The conversations which constitute the bulk of this book took place over the spring and summer of 2000. They were carried out with three main aims in mind.

First, the conversations were held to give Zygmunt Bauman an opportunity to outline some of the deep currents beneath the surfaces of the many texts with which he has changed the nature of a significant proportion of contemporary social thought.

Second, the conversations sought to provide a context in which Bauman could explore some of his ideas in a relatively relaxed manner and, thereby, summarize what he takes to be some of the key concerns of the body of work that bears his name.

Third, the conversations were held to enable Bauman to reflect upon the meanings which his texts have come to possess, as they have spun out of the control of the author and come to take on what amounts to a life of their own.

If this book achieves any of those aims it will have succeeded admirably and, hopefully, it will therefore encourage new generations of social thinkers to go to Bauman's books for themselves and grapple with their challenges, insights and inspirations.

Zygmunt Bauman's work is, to say the least, voluminous and its quantity increases at a prodigious rate. Furthermore, the English-language work for which Bauman is best known was preceded by a number of books and essays which he wrote in his native Poland, before his expulsion in 1968. It would have been a foolish task for these conversations to attempt to summarize and reflect upon the complete body of his work. Consequently, the book focuses mostly on Bauman's 'English period' work. It must also be noted that these conversations took place during a specific moment in Bauman's intellectual career, at a time when his ground-breaking concern with postmodernity was being replaced with a new orientation of his thought around a conception of 'liquid modernity', at a time when certain of the ethical commitments which make his work so distinctive were being reconfigured through conceptions of politics and justice.

It is necessary to make it perfectly clear that Zygmunt Bauman exercised (and sought) no control over the questions I asked, and neither did he make any attempt (nor did he wish) to influence the comments on his work which I offer in the introduction (and for which I alone am responsible).

Zygmunt Bauman displayed an extraordinary good humour, friendliness and warmth during the putting together of this book. As ever, I would like to acknowledge the considerable debts I owe to him. I would also like to thank Ross Abbinnett, Chris Shilling and John Thompson for their good advice.

Keith Tester

Introduction

It will be useful to organize this introduction by asking and answering three questions. Who is Zygmunt Bauman? What does he do? Why does he do it? Needless to say, an introduction of this length cannot pay any adequate attention to the breadth and complexity of Bauman's thought. I do not pretend that it can. The aim of this introduction is very modest. It seeks simply to provide *a* way into Bauman's social thought for those who are unfamiliar with it. Reading Bauman's books is not comforting but it does make you think differently about the world, yourself and, perhaps most importantly of all, your relationships to and with others.

Who is Zygmunt Bauman?

One way of answering the first question is to refer to one of the claims that have been made about Bauman's work. It has been said that he is 'one of the most interesting and influential commentators on . . . our human condition'. That quotation is from Dennis Smith's biography of Bauman, and Smith also thinks that 'Bauman is part of the story he tells' (Smith 1999: 3). Smith's point is that Bauman's books and essays are one of the most significant bodies of work for understanding the nature of the world in which we live, and that Bauman is an especially keen observer of the key trends and forces of the present because he has experienced them in an especially sharp way.

Smith speculates that many of Bauman's intellectual concerns reflect his life experiences. This is going too far, but the nub of the point is well made. It is hard to imagine that Bauman's experiences have had *no* impact upon the themes and temper of his social thought. Bauman was born into a poor Jewish family in Poland in 1925. With his family he fled to the Soviet Union from the Nazi invasion of Poland in September 1939. There, he joined the Polish Army and fought on the Russian Front. Bauman started an academic career in the early 1950s, and was a professor at the University of Warsaw until he was exiled during an anti-Semitic campaign by the Communist authorities in 1968. He became Professor of Sociology at the University of Leeds in 1971, where he remained until his formal retirement in 1990. One point which it is worth pulling out of this biographical sketch is the fact that when Bauman writes in English he is writing in what is at least his *third* language (having been born in Poland and schooled in the Soviet Union).

It is too tempting to relate Bauman's social thought to this biography. For example, he has written a number of articles about his native Poland and about problems of the transition from Communism to a kind of capitalism, themes which also appear in some of his books (see, for example, Bauman 1988). He has written about totalitarianism and, in particular, the Holocaust (Bauman 1989, 1991). The characters of the vagabond and tourist who feature in his studies of postmodernity could be taken to reflect his own experiences of forced exiles (Bauman 1992a, 1993, 1995, 1997). Finally, it might even be argued that his commitment to an ethics of care which ought to endure over the long term and irrespective of fleeting personal preferences reflects his own desire to re-embed himself in a world which only provides travel cots (Bauman 1998a, 2000a). Yes, all of that is tempting, but there are at least three major problems if we reduce

Bauman's – or for that matter any other social thinker's – themes and concerns to questions of biography. First, if it is argued that Bauman's work reflects his personal experiences we are logically required to make much the same claim for the work of everyone else. If that is a move we are prepared to carry out, we have to end up concluding that all social thought is autobiography and that, since all autobiographies tend to keep some incidents quiet and build up others, all social thought consists in little more than what the thinkers prefer to say about themselves. If we are still prepared to continue with this line of thought, we are ultimately required to say that questions of morality, oppression, freedom, suffering, happiness, pleasure can be entirely reduced to the individual and that they have no general importance whatsoever. Or, put another way, the very possibility of social thought collapses, as does, more importantly, the idea that the lives of men and women are in some way intertwined. We end up with that old slogan from a recent dark age for human kindness, 'there is no such thing as society.'

Second, if we explain Bauman's thought by reference to his biography we are actually making ourselves completely incapable of understanding what he has to say. Bauman's work can be difficult enough without making the job of interpretation even harder by beginning from an unsatisfactory basis. As Peter Beilharz has noted, Bauman 'does not like to talk about his life's path' (Beilharz 2000: 3; to this extent the biographical information which is provided in the first conversation of this book is remarkable and sufficient for the purposes of understanding the relationship of Bauman's life to his thought). This is for good sociological and moral reasons. And those reasons are outlined by Richard Sennett, a thinker Bauman greatly admires. In his magnificent book, *The Fall of Public Man*, Sennett develops an argument which says that contemporary culture has eroded public life to such an extent that the boundary between the public and the private has been destroyed. In our culture, we do not say that someone is 'good' because they are civil or courteous in public but, instead, we seek to know every-thing about them. Public life has been replaced with a desire for intimacy; we want intimate knowledge and a feeling that we 'really know' whoever it is. Their private lives and peccadillos become standards by which we measure their worth. We become absorbed by what they do rather than who they are. Sennett says, 'In such a society, the test of whether people are being authentic and "straight" with each other is a peculiar standard of market exchange in intimate relations' (1986: 8). We are taken to be good and honest people if we are prepared to tell everyone anything. Proof of this observation is all around: in the chat shows which fill up the chasms of daytime television, in blockbuster biogra-phies of the safely dead, in the 'cult of celebrity' which dominates popular culture. But Sennett's point is that this kind of culture signals the end of public life since it deprives us of having anything in common other than our secrets, lies and intrusiveness. Similarly, Bauman's refusal to talk about himself is nothing less than a refusal to indulge in this game. It is a practical repudiation of this cultural expectation and the costs it inflicts upon people. Bauman eschews the auto-biographical so that *public* life – the only kind of life which can be the foundation of a principled and respectful *politics* – can be bolstered and practised instead.

Third, the biography which *is* central to Zygmunt Bau-man's social thought is that of his wife, Janina. At a first glance this might seem to be an odd comment to make because it flies in the face of the lesson which is taught by Richard Sennett that public life does not demand intimacy with the personal (indeed that a public life is impossible if it is collapsed into intimacies of the personal). But the sugges-tion that Janina Bauman's experiences are important to Zygmunt Bauman's social thought is reconcilable with the lesson from Sennett for the simple reason that Janina Bau-man has written a book of memoirs which has clearly had an enormous impact on what Zygmunt Bauman does. The book by Janina Bauman is *Winter in the Morning* (1986), and it recounts her experiences as a Jewish girl living in Warsaw during the full onslaught of the Nazi occupation. Janina Bauman recounts how the warm fabric of her prewar life was torn to shreds, how she was forced with her mother and sister into the Warsaw Ghetto and how they managed to escape deportation to the death camps.

Janina Bauman's book has left traces in Zygmunt Bauman's social thought. It was *Winter in the Morning* which made Zygmunt Bauman appreciate that his own life experiences had to be gone beyond if he were to be able to study the Holocaust, which he interprets as a crystallization of the tendencies and possibilities of modernity. Zygmunt Bauman had, of course, escaped the Nazi occupation (he mentions his meetings with Nazis in our first conversation) and therefore his own experiences were not sufficient to the problem. In the preface to *Modernity and the Holocaust* he wrote, 'Having read Janina's book, I began to think just how much I did not know – or rather, did not think about properly. It dawned on me that I did not really understand what had happened in that "world which was not mine"' (1989: vii; the last few words in that quotation are themselves in quotation marks because they refer to the acknowledgements page of *Winter in the Morning*). The Holocaust was part of *someone else's* story. Clearly then, the practice of social thought requires that we go beyond our own lives and subordinate that story to something publicly more important (a position which resonates with the methodological statements which are made in Bauman 1978, and the ethical arguments which run through his work on postmodernity; the issue is to live *for the other*).

In sum then, if a person wishes to write of their biography, that is one thing. But it is something quite different for others to do it on their behalf, in terms of a cultural expectation that 'this is what everyone will want to know.' As Bauman's own sociology of the burdens of identity in modernity, postmodernity and liquid modernity reveals (Bauman 2000b), there is an admirable dignity about a morally rigorous personal privacy (a privacy which is moral precisely because it always respects the dignity of other

people). Bauman shows that the *work* of the sociologist is –
or ought to be – publicly more important than the *life* of the
sociologist. Public relevance does not demand that we are
bared in the public arena. And if contemporary expectations
do so demand, well, as Bauman's sociology demonstrates,
perhaps that is one fashion that we must resist at all costs.
To give in to that pressure is to play a part in the devastation
of public life and, therefore, politics.

So: who is Zygmunt Bauman? For us, he is a private man
who invites participation in public life.

What does Zygmunt Bauman do?

The second question is easy to ask, but difficult to answer.
The answer depends on where we look. If we look at
Bauman's books, it quickly becomes clear that what Bauman
does is write enormously quickly and with a remarkable
ability to focus on the exact issue that pulls together many
of the otherwise divergent problems and issues of the present. At this level, it might be said that Bauman performs a
role of *translation*. He synthesizes what is going on and what
is important, and presents it to social thinkers so that they
can pursue the debates for themselves. Bauman translates
the world into texts. He is not a systems builder and neither
does Bauman's social thought consist in the relentless picking away at a single conceptual or thematic scab. He is an
essayist through whom the present comes to make some
kind of coherent sense.

Perhaps it is only because the world of social thought
finally believes that it is catching up with Bauman that his
work is beginning to move out of the footnotes and into the
mainstream. However, the irony is that as soon as Bauman is
'hooked' in this way, the academic anglers will only discover
that actually he has slipped away to explore different waters.
Consequently, if we want to understand what Zygmunt
Bauman does it is appropriate to look elsewhere than at

some 'key concepts'. It is better to look at the deeper waters
of his thought. And, if we do that, we will see that 'what
Bauman does' can be summarized relatively coherently.
By admission and temperament what Bauman does is
sociology. Bauman is a sociologist – and he identifies himself
as such – because, as he explains in the first of these
conversations, he believes that sociology is more capable
than any other academic discipline of capturing and embracing the entirety of human experience. He argues that human
experience does not respect firm boundaries between the
social, the political, the economic or the poetic, and neither
does sociology. In this way, sociology is a unique discipline,
and what many commentators might identify as its terminal
weakness (its tendency to take on board ideas from elsewhere, its inability to build up high walls between itself and,
say, politics or philosophy) is, in fact, its profound strength.
    This is a theme that has been a constant in Bauman's
thought through the years. Although the prose style is a lot
more dense than will be expected by readers who are only
familiar with the books that Bauman has written since the
late 1970s, such an all-embracing understanding of the
stakes and importance of sociology can be found in an essay
from the 1960s in which it was contended that 'to understand man we have to bring together all that we have
discovered while penetrating the different aspects of his
unified life-process.' In that essay, Bauman went on to make
it clear that the word 'unified' was being used in a specific
way, contrary to commonsense usage. After all, 'the word
implies something which is brought together after having
been divided; what we have in mind however is the kind of
unity existing before any division took place' (Bauman 1969:
1). Accordingly, although Bauman is a sociologist, he is a
sociologist of a peculiar kind. He believes that disciplinary
boundaries are to be treated with suspicion and even ignored
in the search for a more all-embracing and relevant knowledge of the social world.
    What Bauman does, then, is sociology under the sign of
eclecticism and catholicity. But this is not an eclecticism of

self-aggrandizement or self-preening. It is an eclecticism made necessary by the fact that human life is itself fundamentally wide-ranging, diverse and impossible to capture under any single heading. Bauman is saying that we need an open-ended kind of sociology in order to be up to the task of understanding the open-endedness of the lives of men and women. Undoubtedly, this is the reason why Bauman's work manages to appeal to so many people who are engaged in what might be generally called 'social thought' and why his books have managed to move beyond the narrower confines of 'sociology' as it is conventionally understood.

One interesting implication of this understanding of sociology (of Bauman's understanding of what he does) is that it can explain one of the curious moments in this book. In the first conversation, I ask Zygmunt Bauman which book he would take with him to a desert island: if he could only take one book what would it be? I was expecting the answer to be Gramsci's *Prison Notebooks*, Weber's *The Protestant Ethic and the Spirit of Capitalism* or, more probably, Simmel's *The Philosophy of Money*. Instead, Bauman listed a number of works of literature and in the end decided upon a short story by the Argentine writer, Jorge Luis Borges. This was a surprise but, in the light of Bauman's distinctive understanding of the stakes of sociology, it can be explained. From Bauman's point of view, a short story by Borges possesses as much sociological relevance and insight as any text that might be more readily accepted as part of the 'canon'. Indeed, a short story by Borges might be more useful than conventional sociology books if it is better able to capture in an all-embracing way the flux and open-endedness of the social lives of men and women. However, while the link of sociology with literature in Bauman's thought is extremely suggestive (and can help explain why he so often refers to literature in his books), it is important not to press the link too far. When all is said and done, Bauman's books are undeniably instances of social thought. What Bauman does is practise and promote thought about the relationships, situations and forces which are experienced and confronted by men and women and, importantly, experienced by them as being *real*. Literature might well be able to cast new and challenging light on these relationships, situations and forces (especially if the literature is like that of some of Bauman's favourite authors: Robert Musil, Milan Kundera, Georges Perec), but the fact remains that it is built up on the basis of the *fictional* and not the experientially and socially *factual*.

But there is another way of answering the question 'What does Bauman do?' Yes, he 'does' sociology but, within that field, he tries to do something which is important in itself. Within his sociology, Bauman tries to show that the world does not have to be the way it is and that there is an alternative to what presently seems to be so natural, so obvious, so inevitable. This concern betrays the mark of two of the key influences on the development of Bauman's social thought: the post-Leninist Marxism of Antonio Gramsci and the sociology of Georg Simmel. The way in which these two figures have influenced Bauman is made clear in a conversation which he held with Peter Beilharz (see Beilharz 2001: 334–44).

There, Bauman said that what Gramsci did was show him that men and women are not the unthinking dupes of social structures which determine everything, and neither are they (that is to say, we) little more than beings who move only when we react to external stimulation. Instead, Gramsci showed that men and women are agents in their own right. For Bauman, having read Gramsci, it was possible to appreciate that men and women are possessed of the ability and the power to make the world for themselves. Gramsci showed that it is only because of the 'common sense' that is promoted by the prevailing ordering structures that this potential is neither glimpsed nor acted upon. Gramsci showed Bauman that things can be different, and that there are alternatives which can be made by men and women. This was an influence which sat – and continues to sit – very easily with Bauman's understanding of culture as a 'knife pressed against the future' (see Bauman 1973, 1999a). In these terms, culture is at once the expression of the realiz-

ation that there is an alternative and an encouragement to
men and women to think differently, in unauthorized ways,
about the world in which they live, work and die. Moreover,
the insight of Gramsci that the world is something which
can be made by social action and agents enabled Bauman to
break out of the 'official' Soviet-style Communism in which
his thought was trapped during its early years. As the
caffeine which was injected into the intellectual bloodstream
by Gramsci started to thud into Bauman's brain, it became
clear that the version of Marxism and socialism which was
promoted by the Soviet system was something to be
approached critically and suspiciously, in that it told men
and women that the Party or some abstraction called the
Proletariat or Historical Necessity was the maker of history
and not themselves. As Bauman says in these conversations,
Gramsci enabled him to retain a commitment to the moral
core of Marx's thought while releasing him from the
unthoughts of the Soviet system. (It was in this way that
Bauman became one of the leading thinkers in the wave of
'humanistic Marxism' or 'Marxist revisionism' which
emerged in Poland during the 1950s. For a flavour of that
brand of Marxism, and for interesting parallels with aspects
of Bauman's thought, see Kolakowski 1969, 1978.)

As Bauman has explained (in Beilharz 2001: 334), Gramsci taught him *what* his social thought ought to look at. But
it was Simmel who taught him *how* to look at the world
which has come to seem and feel so natural to men and
women that they cannot conceive of the chance that there
might be an alternative. In the conversation with Peter
Beilharz, Bauman put it this way: 'Simmel took away . . .
the youthful hope/check that once the "surface" incongrui-
ties and contradictions are out of the way, I'll find "down
there" the clockwork running exactly to the second.' Bauman drew a further message from Simmel: 'that for the
pencil of every tendency there is an eraser of another, and
to wish to dismantle that ambivalence in order to see better
how society works is like wishing to take the walls apart to
see better what supports the ceiling' (Bauman in Beilharz

2001: 335). What Simmel showed Bauman is that it is the job of sociology to cast a suspicious eye on any claim that the social world would operate in an orderly way and with a tendency towards a kind of equilibrium if it were not for men and women behaving in such unpredictable and ambivalent ways. Simmel showed that ambivalence and uncertainty are the essence of social life and that it is therefore incumbent upon sociology to try to capture that flux without ever closing it down or wishing it away (and so, once again, we are back to Bauman's distinctive vision of sociology as well as to his principled public persona of someone who will not say what his books 'really mean'). In this light, it is small wonder that Bauman finds little to interest him in Parsonian and post-Parsonian American sociology, with its remorseless emphasis on 'the problem of order'. Bauman would almost certainly object that the problem of order is less a sociological category problem than it is a political and material problem for the men and women who have to endure its everyday consequences.

So: what does Zygmunt Bauman do? He uses an eclectic sociology to show his readers that the world can be different than it is and that, in spite of everything, there is an alternative. But men and women can only act in public if they are not forced into the paralysing straightjacket of displays of ersatz intimacy.

Why does Zygmunt Bauman do it?

In thinking about *what* Bauman does, we have already started to move into an understanding of *why* he does it. He is a social thinker because he wants men and women to make the world for themselves, to press a knife against the future and thus practise freedom rather than accept the constraints of necessity. This is why, at the end of the first conversation, Bauman explains that he has always tried to attend to beauty and humiliation. Beauty is the expression of the human ability to make and think a different world (it is a going beyond the necessities of this world), and humiliation (whether the physical humiliation of suffering or the material humiliation of poverty) is the piling up of necessity over and against possibility (hence Bauman's concern with the human consequences of globalization and with the lot of the 'new poor': Bauman 1998a, 1998b). But there is more to the question 'why?' than even that.

One of the most significant and compelling of the many qualities of Bauman's thought is its moral rigour and seriousness. Unlike many social thinkers, Bauman does not think that questions of morality can be reduced to personal tastes, to the positions and experiences of specific groups, or to methodological procedures. Neither does he believe that questions of morality can be analysed away into something that is supposed to be more fundamental. Instead, Bauman argues (and the argument runs through much of this book) that morality is about commitment to the other over time. Morality is not about temporary whims, it is about humans *as* humans and not humans in so far as they are like me. He believes that morality is the fundamental human issue because we are always and inevitably confronted in our lives with other people in the general and a few significant others in the particular. For Bauman then, social thought is indivisibly moral in its content and concerns. It is about *humanity*.

This aspect of his work was clarified for Zygmunt Bauman by Janina Bauman's *Winter in the Morning*. Janina Bauman wrote that 'the cruellest thing about cruelty is that it dehumanizes its victims before it destroys them. And . . . the hardest of struggles is to remain human in inhuman conditions' (1986: x). This is a phrase that summarizes much of the ethical vision which is at the heart of Zygmunt Bauman's sociology (it can certainly be read as the dominant theme of *Modernity and the Holocaust*, 1989). He looks at how social orders are complicit in dehumanization. But, instead of performing the easy option and throwing up his hands in despair at the inhumanity of it all, Bauman tries to recover the possibility of humanity. The point is that humans do not *have* to be inhuman even if they live in social and historical circumstances which make the cruel treatment of the other seem to be easy and without consequence. It is always possible to choose to be human, it is always possible to choose to be moral. In that choice lies our human dignity. And it is the role of sociology to show that the choice to be moral can always be made since all the structures and thoughts which tell us that the choice is impossible are themselves entirely contingent.

Social thought is *for* humanity. In the Beilharz conversation, Bauman explained that 'from Janina I learned that *Wertfreiheit* [value freedom] is – as human sciences are concerned – not just a pipe-dream, but also an utterly inhuman delusion; that sociologizing makes sense only in as far as it helps humanity in life, that in the ultimate account it is the human choices that make all the difference between lives human and inhuman.' And then followed the insight which takes this focus on the choices which lead to the human or the inhuman *sociological* rather than *philosophical*: 'and that society is an ingenious contraption to narrow down, perhaps eliminate altogether, those choices' (Bauman in Beilharz 2001: 335). This is *sociological* because it means that if we want to understand the qualities of what it means to be human today, we must attend to the situations in which humans are to be found. Moreover, in so far as they are tied to a sociological way of thinking, these moral commitments and claims of Zygmunt Bauman are removed from speculation and become measures by which humiliation and suffering in the world can be known and named for what it is – the product of evil. Bauman feels no need to justify his moral commitments. Instead it is the world which must justify itself in terms of the critique which those commitments make necessary. Bauman is suspicious of the world and what it means for men and women. He is *not* suspicious about men and women and their ability to choose to be moral (that is, to choose to be human).

All of this might make it seem as if Bauman sees sociology

as a political platform or movement. He does not. Bauman does not do sociology because he believes that sociologists are the people who can finally set the world to rights and ensure that all people live in peace and harmony. He explicitly rejects this sort of interpretation of the reasons why sociology ought to be done (see, for example, Bauman 1987). Instead, Bauman ties the practice of sociology to values which stand beyond it and which speak to all men and women and not just to the community of social thinkers. Bauman is motivated by an unqualified respect for humanity. He is committed to the dignity of humanity.

This is a dignity which consists in transcending the humiliations of the everyday and, to the contrary, striving, in practice and imagination, to make an alternative that is fit for humanity. Sociology is an important agent in making this reimagining and repractising possible in that it deprives the prevailing structures, relationships and institutions of the air of invulnerability that they so desperately need. But what that striving needs is a public space in which people can come together without fear that all their hopes and ambitions will be shot down because of the public desire for intimacy with the private person. We can only hope and desire if we are confident: confident in our material security, confident in our selves. And so, once again, we return full circle to the principled reasons why Zygmunt Bauman steadfastly refuses to make the private individual more important than the public persona.

So: why does Zygmunt Bauman do it? Because he is committed to humanity.

Conclusion

Hopefully, it is now possible to understand a little of the stakes and character of Zygmunt Bauman's social thought. The conversations in this book should help to push that understanding a lot further and, indeed, clarify the currents beneath the surface of his texts. One thing that should be very clear is that, beneath the surfaces of the books which are so good at capturing the essence of the present, Bauman's work is guided – and I would suggest has *always* been guided – by a deep and unflinching commitment to *humanity*. That commitment has taken different forms at different times but it has never disappeared. This is something Zygmunt Bauman has never lost sight of. And it is this commitment which makes his voice so distinctive, challenging and significant. The commitment is fundamental to how we can understand who Bauman is, what he does and why he does it.

But there is one final lesson that Zygmunt Bauman's social thought teaches. He teaches the virtue of *dedication* despite and in the face of the allures of temporary distractions. The commitment to humanity itself requires a commitment of the self. Towards the end of his inaugural lecture at the University of Leeds in 1972, Bauman said that: 'more than ever we must beware of falling into the traps of fashion which may well prove much more detrimental than the malaise they claim to cure. Well, our vocation, after all these unromantic years, may become again a testfield of courage, consistency, and loyalty to human values' (Bauman 1972: 203).

Zygmunt Bauman teaches what the vocation publicly demands of the social thinker, how it ought to be pursued and, most importantly of all, why it is worth the effort.

Keith Tester

Conversation 1

Context and Sociological Horizons

KEITH TESTER *You started a sociological career in Poland in the early 1950s. Presumably, in Poland at that time, sociology was part of a wider project of, by declared aims at least, attempting to make a world fit for humans after the wreckage of the Nazi Occupation. There must have been a sense that sociology could help change the world (a sensibility that I, as a sociologist in a very different situation, have never been able to uphold; I have never been able to believe that sociology could change the world). Could you say something about sociology in the Polish context and, more personally, why you chose sociology rather than, say, philosophy, aesthetics, engineering. Put simply: Sociology in Poland in the early fifties. What was it for and what roads led you to it?*

ZYGMUNT BAUMAN   You may say that from early childhood on I was shuttled from one pair of rails to another, each one presumably going somewhere, but each pointing in a different direction. There is perhaps a metanarrative that would make that wriggling between trajectories look like a trajectory in its own right. But to insist that there *is* one would mean stretching our romance with logic really too far.

Sometimes, over a drink, I play with Janina a game of imagination. What would have happened to either of us were there to have been no Hitler and no war? To start with, we would probably have never met. And if we had, we would have hardly been allowed to marry: there was a class barrier between us too high to be negotiated in prewar Poland. I would have got nowhere near a higher education either. As a child, I was considered a hard-working pupil and I was an avid reader (I was then, as I still am, fully and truly enthralled by the richness of Polish culture and literature; my love was however bound to remain unrequited), but I would not have been admitted into Polish universities as they strictly observed the *numerus clausus* or even *numerus nullus* rule regarding Jewish applicants, and – being poor – my parents were not able to finance my study abroad as was common among affluent Polish Jews. Would I have become a sociologist then? Most certainly, I would not have been an academic.

From 1 September 1939 on, there was but shuffling between itineraries, a seemingly unending series of 'disembeddings' with beds moving too fast for 're-embedding'. The stone stopped rolling, or at least slowed down considerably, only in 1971 when we stopped in Leeds ('settling' there took longer). The funny thing is that I am more like a cat than a dog. I tend to develop attachment to a place rather than following the caprices of a restless master. Were I in a position to choose, I would be telling you now an altogether different story (that is, if you were interested in my story in such a case).

Unlike Janina, I managed to escape the Nazi Occupation and my only personal encounters with the Nazis (a few years after the invasion of Poland) were through the barrel of a gun. When I was in the deep north of Russia I dreamed of becoming a physicist. I even managed to take the first two years of a course (through correspondence: as a 'Westerner' I was not allowed into large cities where universities were located). I did not think much of sociology then – nor was there much of a sociology to think of – in Stalin's Russia.

Once I had volunteered to join the Polish army which was formed in the USSR, physics had to be put on a side burner, and there it stayed until it fizzled out altogether. Other things grasped my imagination. With the army, I fought my way back to a country devastated by a war which only aggravated its prewar misery and backwardness. To lift it from penury and centuries-long retardation was an exciting task. But the new powers promised more, much more than that: the end to discrimination, petty enmities and the day-to-day cruelty of people suffocating in a country which did not have enough work for them to make sense of their lives and not enough bread to keep them alive. It promised an *equality of dignified life* to all, more than enough to make a nineteen-year-old, just returned from the woods and the front-line, breathless. Should time be wasted fathoming mysteries of big bangs and black holes? Let other black holes keep their mysteries for a while – first came my country in ruins and the big bang of its resurrection.

You say that you never believed that sociology could change the world. Well, I did (and I cannot swear that I've lost my faith by now, though I have changed radically my view of the way in which the job of changing could, and should, be performed). Yes, sociology was, as you say, 'part of a wider project', and the project was to conjure up human conditions in which the humans could live as humans would.

I joined Warsaw University at an inopportune moment though, in the midst of a brief, yet no less nasty for that, episode of 'Stalinization'. Stalinization never went as far in Poland as in other countries in the Soviet orbit, but far enough to suspend the courses offered by the luminaries of prewar social science (most painfully, those of Stanislaw Ossowski). I took my MA exams in philosophy, but soon the 'old guard' returned and sociology was given full academic status. It also moved quickly into the centre of public interest. 'Society' mattered to everybody, regardless of political sympathies: it was ages before Peter Drucker's summary of the Reaganized/Thatcherized 'public opinion' ('No more salvation by society'). People needed salvation badly, and whatever colour or shape salvation was to take, it could only *come from society*. Of that society, sociology was to tell the truth. The first issue of the thick and ponderous academic quarterly *Sociological Studies* [*c.*1961], of which I was the founder and first editor, was sold out on the first day of publication from street kiosks.

In the total absence of 'another opinion', let alone a contrary opinion, and in particular an articulated contrary position, information about the state of affairs in Polish society or any sector of it was 'the truth'. Truth is an agonistic concept, you come to appreciate its privileged status only in a contest and in the face of a challenge. Defending our 'data' against continuous attacks from the Party hierarchy infuriated by the sheer fact that some people somewhere claimed an independent story-telling authority, made it all too easy for us to believe that what we announced was, indeed, *the truth*. And so believed the rest of the 'enlightened public'. This unearned status of truth-umpire secured for sociology an unbelievably high volume of prestige. In the end, it proved to be demoralizing: any scrap of information passing under the name of sociology, however miserable, vacuous or sloppy, was received with awe and public applause. The threshold had been lowered, it was not clear what was good and what bad sociology. And the coming of a free opinion market later on took sociologists, brought up in a sort of perverse greenhouse, unprepared, and for many it was a traumatic experience. In the 1950s, the uncertainties born of the multiplicity of authorities were, though, matters of a distant, hardly anticipated future, not much different from a figment of fantasy going wild.

In the past you have spoken about two of your teachers, Stanislaw Ossowski and Julian Hochfeld. It might not be far-fetched to say that they are two of the keys to understanding your social thought. And yet they are more or less completely unknown in the West. Consequently, a significant aspect of your intellectual context is utterly mysterious to many of your readers. Could you say something about Ossowski and Hochfeld, their work and their example?

Once the 'Stalinization' episode ended, the Department of Philosophy and Sociology at Warsaw University became a powerful centre of thought, in which all strands of the manifold traditions of sociology were brought under the same roof and engaged in mutual conversation. In this quality it was truly unique in the East and the West alike. I am tempted to say that it was, simultaneously, 'behind' and 'ahead' of academic centres of sociology of the time. When, in the late fifties, I started visiting foreign places, I was struck by how one-sided and narrowly profiled in comparison were the visions of sociology taught elsewhere. Where else but at Warsaw were the Marxist and positivist traditions, scientistic and humanistic sociologies, evolutionist and structuralist approaches, 'naturalist' and 'culturalist' visions of social reality, statistical and hermeneutic strategies, taught side by side, as live alternatives, complementary rather than mutually exclusive, and free of the chronopolitical straightjacket? The understanding of sociology with which my teachers at Warsaw inoculated me was one of ongoing and far from finished discourse, self-scrutiny and continuous recapitulation. The history of social thought appeared to me to be full of precious gems, with the job of cutting and polishing them still ahead. I was amazed (and put off!) to find sociological tradition being taught the 'Whig history' way, as the story of human folly, the gallant war against ignorance and prejudices, and the juxtaposition of scientific truth, one and indivisible, with a variegated mass of curios and errors of primitive minds.

I am so grateful to Ossowski and Hochfeld for having vaccinated me, at the very beginning of my sociological life and once and for all, against the idea that sociology is (or should become) a kind of physics which leaves its own history behind and never looks back, and that, if sociology has not yet quite reached that level, it is because of its 'immaturity' or failure to discover the right and proper research methodology which will put paid to controversy and doubt. What I learned from them was that sociology has no other – and cannot have any other – sense (and no other utility either) than of an ongoing commentary on human 'lived experience', as transient and obsessively self-updating as that experience itself. What I admired in both of them was a mixture of the passionate ambition to understand, and the humility arising from realization that the task of understanding is unlikely ever to be completed: but also the conviction that it is precisely that awareness of incompleteness which makes the sociologist's learned commentary helpful to people struggling daily with the challenges of life. Much, much later I came across Franz Rosenzweig's distinction between 'abstract' and 'speaking' thinking. The 'abstract' thinker knows his truth in advance, he thinks for no one else and speaks for no one else, while the 'speaking' thinker cannot anticipate anything and must wait for the word of the Other. He speaks to someone who has not only ears but also a mouth. When it starts, speech does not know where it will end: it takes its cues from others. I read these words, and I had the uncanny feeling of *déjà vu*. These words seemed to me to encapsulate my teachers' teachings, and they taught me to stand steadfastly on the 'speaking thinking' side.

Both Ossowski and Hochfeld, their numerous differences notwithstanding, were politically socialist, and in their scholarly work inspired by ethical motives. I guess that they found the prime sense of sociological vocation in the fact that humans suffer and that seeing through the social causes of their suffering may help them to mitigate their misery or even make the social production of misery grind to a halt. A mixture of disaffection and hope. I am not sure that they believed that thought may change the world, but most certainly they took it for granted that the world can be different than it is, but it won't change without self-scrutiny and reflection. If, as J.B. Cabell (an American novelist) suggested, the optimist proclaims we live in the best of all possible worlds while the pessimist fears this is true, Ossowski and Hochfeld were neither in the optimist nor in the pessimist camp; just where the sociologist worth her salt should be.

It is a pity that thinkers of that calibre have made little impact outside Polish borders. Ossowski's profound phenomenological inquiry into class and stratification systems as 'thinking models' has been translated into English, but grossly underrated. It was received as, mostly, a political curiosity: a book critical of Marxism emerging from a Marxist country. His other works in social psychology, sociology of art, the study of culture, have never been translated, and neither is his programmatic work on the sociological vocation available in English. Of Hochfeld's work, only scattered essays, published in not widely read periodicals, are available in English (but not his magnificent study of the springs and pitfalls of revolution, written around Rosa Luxemburg's famous pamphlet). This is a great pity, and Western sociology's great loss. And yet a 'teacher' is more than a lecturer or writer, and I doubt whether Ossowski's and Hochfeld's greatness as teachers would be fully grasped from their books. It was my good fortune indeed to spend my formative years looking up to them for instruction and inspiration.

What were the 'key texts' and who were the 'key thinkers' in your initial development as a sociologist? More specifically, what did you draw from the classical social thinkers: Marx, Durkheim, Weber and Simmel? Perhaps I can also ask you the 'Desert Island Discs' question. You are marooned on the island and you can take one book with you: what is it?

I do not remember the concept of the 'classic' (or for that matter 'founding father of sociology') being applied selectively to the Marx–Weber–Durkheim triad or any other chosen individuals in my student years, as was to become a habit later, largely under the influence of Talcott Parsons. Each kind of sociology weaves its own etiological myths and conjures up its own forefathers; it also chooses the way its ancestors are selected and the significance attached to that selection. Parsons's struggle to rewrite the history of sociology as an unbroken line of progress ending in the all-embracing and ultimate Parsonian synthesis was an intellectual gloss on the (fortunately soon to be dashed) bid for a church-like theoretical domination, and such a bid needed its saints and required a Pantheon of strictly controlled composition. An invitingly open sociology suspicious of, and resistant to, all monopoly claims has no need to split the lore into the canon and the apocrypha. Warsaw sociology certainly did not. When the winds blowing from the other coast of the Atlantic brought the news of canonization, they found Ossowski and Hochfeld, unlike some of their ears-pricking younger colleagues, largely indifferent, as a rule critical, and if need be trying hard to fight back the new fashion for which they did not have much use.

For better or worse, I've never come to understand what (apart, that is, from historical contingencies) is so special in Weber's or Durkheim's work (or in other work for that matter) which would justify ascribing to them a separate and privileged status in the rich and expanding tradition of social thought, to the detriment of other ingredients which contributed to its continuing liveliness and fertility. I saw Durkheim in a long line of 'sociologistic sociologists' stretching from Montesquieu, Diderot, Rousseau, through Claude Saint-Simon and Auguste Comte up to Mauss, Halbwachs. Weber belonged to another line, which included Dilthey, Windelband and Rickert, but also for instance Werner Sombart. And there was a wide panoply of great Polish social thinkers which included virtually any past and present way of doing sociology: Gumplowicz, Kelles-Kraus, Krzywicki, Czarnowski, Znaniecki . . .

I suspect that failing to learn respect and reverence for 'canonical texts' (a trained inability which extends to my relations with present-day celebrities) has been my original sin in the eyes of the model academic. That failure did not make my academic life easier: I was never any good in the art of exegesis, in 'sticking to the letter' of hallowed texts, and it barred me from ever being admitted to any school or caucus. In any established company I was out of place. But in exchange it gave me the kind of freedom which I would not trade off for the comforts of belonging: freedom to draw from any source which I find inspiring, and draw as much as I find worthy of being drawn.

Which brings me to your 'desert island' question. It would

be a tall order for me to decide between Robert Musil's *The Man Without Qualities*, Georges Perec's *Life: A User's Manual*, Jorge Luis Borges' *Labyrinths* and Italo Calvino's *Invisible Cities*. These books exemplify everything I learned to desire and struggled, in vain, to attain: the breadth of vistas, the at-homeness in all compartments of the treasury of human thought, the sense of the many-facetedness of human experience and sensitivity to its as-yet-undiscovered possibilities – the style of thinking, and writing, I'd dearly wish to master but alas never did nor will. If pressed to limit my choices, I'd probably settle for Borges' 'The Garden of Forking Paths'.

During the mid-1950s you spent time in England, at the London School of Economics. This must have been a jarring experience both intellectually and politically. On the one hand the kind of sociology that was practised in Poland must have been rather different from what the discipline meant at the LSE and, on the other hand, you must have been struck by the very different problems and possibilities which confronted sociologists in Poland and Britain at that time.

I came to the LSE shortly after the barricades of the 'Polish October' had been dismantled and Wladyslaw Gomulka trumpeted the retreat from the ideal of a free and pluralist society which the nation had hoped he would fulfil (the concept of 'socialism with a human face' had not yet been coined).[1] I already had a study of British socialism (mostly J.S. Mill and the Fabians), my Ph.D. dissertation, behind me, as well as a shorter, yet for me quite seminal, study in the sociology of the Party (the very idea of the Party as an object of sociological scrutiny was blasphemous and criminal) and the logic of bureaucracy. I knew our hopes had been dashed, and was eager to find out what went wrong and where our mistake lay. Hence the study of the dialectics of the social movement and its elite, to which the year spent at the LSE (mostly in its splendid library, my greatest London discovery – free access to bookshelves, and how densely filled!) was entirely dedicated. I made a few acquaintances and struck up a few friendships (most notably, with Ralph Miliband), attended Oakeshott's, Glass's, Titmuss's and Ginsberg's lectures, but socialized mostly with the books. I developed a genuine attachment to Robert McKenzie, my LSE supervisor. I tremendously enjoyed his seminars, to which one acting politician after another was brought to be grilled, and admired his versatile, sceptical but serious, view of the arcane fashions in which the 'cunning of reason' blazed its way through the inanities of political practices.

Shocks? Well, it was during the year at LSE that I was told that sociology has its classics, and I was amazed by what I heard. Also, I found out that one can be a teacher of sociology without fathoming the history of philosophy and social thought, or for that matter roaming the vast expanses of culture, and again I was amazed. I concentrated too intensely, though, on my research and writing to have much time left for these or other shocks.

It is well known that you became disenchanted with the Communist regime in Poland and that by the late 1950s you were playing a part in the development of what most commentators call a 'humanistic Marxism'. What role did Gramsci's thought play in this process? You have previously emphasized his importance to your intellectual development.

To put it in a nutshell, I owe to Gramsci an 'honourable discharge' from Marxist orthodoxy. I do not regret the years of my fascination with Marx's ideas. I learned from Marx, or was inspired by him to develop, cognitive and evaluative frames which I hope are still mine to this very day: disgust for all forms of socially produced injustice, the urge to debunk the lies in which the social responsibility for human misery tends to be wrapped and thus removed from view, and the inclination to smell a rat whenever a clamp on human freedom is contemplated or justified. I guess I came through Marx to my belief in the infinity and perpetual incompleteness of human potential.

If there was a disenchantment, it concerned the ossified form which the 'official' vulgate version of Marxism was given, and more than anything else the official bar on applying Marxist critique to 'really existing socialism', coupled with effacing or playing down the ethical core and source of Marxist teachings. In a paradoxical way Gramsci saved me from turning into an anti-Marxist, as so many other disenchanted thinkers did, throwing out on their way everything that was, and remained, precious and topical in Marx's legacy. I read good tidings in Gramsci's *Prison Notebooks*: there was a way of saving the ethical core, and the analytical potential I saw no reason to discard from the stiff carapace in which it had been enclosed and stifled.

Well, I presume one could learn such truths from other people, or even discover them on one's own. But frankly speaking, to a person like me, trying hard to stay inside the *Weltanschauung* in which I came to feel at home, the fact that the hint came from a thinker whose Marxist credentials even officialdom's stalwarts did not dare to question certainly helped. And the encounter with the *Prison Notebooks* could not have come at a better moment of my life: I had, so to speak, 'matured' with their ingestion and absorption.

In his book The Sociological Imagination, *C. Wright Mills says that parts of two of the chapters were delivered as lectures at the Polish Academy of Sciences in Warsaw in the late 1950s. In the first of these chapters Mills says that sociology should stand up for the values of reason and freedom and thus stand against the tide (which he perceptively calls 'post-modern') of the reduction of the human subject to a 'cheerful robot'. In the second he declares that the sociologist should make the powerful responsible for the consequences of their actions and show the public how their personal worries are connected with the public issues that the powerful create. In so doing, sociology promotes democracy. Now, at the time you were a member of staff at the University of Warsaw. I therefore assume that you were present at Mills's talks, if not, indeed, instrumental in making them happen. What impact did he have? What was the nature of the dialogue between 'Eastern' and 'Western' sociologists at that time?*

Mills's reception in Warsaw was mixed. Many sought his company and found him addressing their thoughts and cravings. Others, dazzled and enamoured by whatever stood for 'American sociology', were nonplussed and embarrassed. Mills did not represent that sociology. On the contrary, at that time Mills baiting was a favourite pastime among the most distinguished members of American academe: there were no expedients, however dishonest, which the ringleaders of the hue-and-cry would consider below their dignity and to which they would not stoop. Mills, after all, was a thorn in the flesh of the thoroughly conformist sociological establishment, having assaulted, one by one, every single one of its sacred cows. He was deviance incarnate, the critic of the American creed among its preachers and admirers. No wonder that to some of my colleagues, about to embark on a Rockefeller or Ford Foundation fellowship, Mills was a sort of Typhoid Mary. Less controversial figures, like Paul Lazarsfeld or Leon Festinger, were greeted with unpolluted enthusiasm (and there were scores of them pilgrimaging to Warsaw at that time, Poland having become after October a veritable Mecca for intellectuals dreaming in vain of 'leading the masses', as well as for those who could not wait for the fall of the Communist enemy). Not Mills though.

People who shirked Mills's company to keep their loyalty to America clean found allies in those who did exactly the same because of their loyalty to the forces of law and order. Proletarians of all countries refused to follow Marx's call, but there seems to be a well-entrenched and thriving International of establishment lovers.

I myself, together with others wishing (and hoping) to humanize our native brand of socialism, read Mills's *The Sociological Imagination* and *The Power Elite* as the story of our own concerns and duties. We did not ask for whom that particular bell tolled. There was a lot that I learned from Mills's books and what I learned was not primarily about

America. The guardians of the Polish regime well knew why the foremost critic of the American power elite should be treated as *persona non grata*.

Let me use Mills's visit, though, to illustrate a point about the mutual comprehension of society's critics being such a tall order. During Mills's stay in Warsaw, Gomulka went on the radio to criticize an essay by my friend Leszek Kolakowski. We all trembled; having our fingers singed so many times before, we expected the worst. But Mills was elated: 'How lucky you are and happy you must be – the leader of the country responding to philosophical tracts! No one at the top pays any attention to what I am doing.'

Your work has been influenced by American social thinkers like Richard Sennett and Christopher Lasch, and Rorty has become one of your major 'stimulants'. But American sociology is largely absent from your books. Could you say something about how you see American sociology?

It is extremely treacherous and utterly unwise to generalize about American sociology. America is a big country and it takes little effort to find ample exceptions to every rule. And yet I must admit that in 'mainstream' American sociology, as represented by the *American Journal of Sociology* for instance, I do not feel at home. Some products I find downright boring, uninspired and uninspiring; others put technical sophistication high above the significance of the issue. On the whole, American sociology developed under the impact of challenges quite different from those faced by European social researchers. For many years it grew in the frame set by warfare and welfare bureaucracies with the intention of responding better to their demands. In my vocabulary, it approached the model of a 'science of unfreedom'. This is quite opposite to my ideal of sociology. Parsons's self-equilibrating 'system' was a thoroughly legitimate culmination of that trend. Even in his most sensible and most 'European' work, *The Structure of Social Action* (it was all the way down after that), the question that set

Parsons's mind in motion was: how can it be that voluntary agents do not behave at random? Nowadays the two frames are crumbling fast (though at different speeds), and many an American sociologist feels as if the link with the 'public agenda' has been lost, and no alternative links have been sufficiently developed. Hence disorientation, and a desperate search for an alternative *raison d'être*. It may not, however, be easy to find it by following the inner logic of the sociological establishment.

For a number of reasons, European sociology seems to be better prepared by its past history to face the challenges of the 'liquid modern' world and make itself useful to its residents. Remember that American society does not have feudalism in its history, nor the anti-feudal revolution, nor *Burgertum* [civil society] and its critics, nor a socialist movement of any real import. Samuel Gompers and his like established trade unions to facilitate the acceptance of migrants in American society, not to wage a class war. On the other hand, Europe never invented a concept of 'anti-European activity'.

I think I should mention that I do not agree with the numerous observers who tend to describe the present-day transformations in Europe (and elsewhere) as a process of 'Americanization'. Nor do I believe that America shows the future of us all. For all sorts of reasons the American model is not universalizable and it is unfit for export. And it takes more, much more, than to eat McDonald's burgers and watch *Friends* and *ER*, or even fall in love with 'zero tolerance' and private prisons, to become 'like America'. And so one can argue that European sociologists should not copy the style, and particularly not the fads and foibles, of their transatlantic namesakes, who are faced with a different kind of society to study, and who have to respond to different challenges.

That answer implicitly raises the issue of the relationship of your own work to European social thought. Your thought seems to fit very much into a peculiarly European tradition of cultural

*critique. For example, Weber wondered if an individual who is
the product of the unique history of the 'Occident' can come to
possess universal understanding; Husserl spoke about the crisis
of the European spirit; Adorno and Horkheimer analysed the
dialectic of Enlightenment and Heller and Feher have identified
Europe as a 'hermeneutic culture'. How do you respond to that
situation of your work?*

Since the concept was coined, Europe was, and still remains,
a *project*. As you know perfectly well, the history of this
north-western peninsula of the Euroasiatic continent was
punctuated by attempts to unite it (more to the point: to
erase inner boundaries or make them irrelevant) over the
heads of the tribes and nations that populated it. Unity must
have seemed, for some reasons, a 'natural fulfilment' of the
European destination. All attempts used military force and
spiritual slogans in varying proportions. And all failed out-
right or proved short-lived, except the one which prudently
abstained from using either force or slogans. The present-
day 'unification of Europe' started from the kitchen rather
than the parlours; talks were conducted about things as
mundane and uncontroversial as coal and steel, and the wise
men like Schumann, Monnet, Adenauer or Spaak who did
the talking never mentioned such nebulous and contentious
words as European culture, spirit or destiny. The present-
day talk about a common European civilization is a follow-
up, a gloss over new, tacitly or even surreptitiously installed,
economic/financial realities. The European Sociology Association was established forty-odd years after the Common
Agricultural Policy and for all I know the latter, however
friable and wobbly, is a paragon of vitality by comparison
with the former.

   What, therefore, is the European sociology? More generally but more relevantly as well, what is 'European culture'?
Many have spoken in its name and yet more will be speaking. And no wonder – since many have the right to do so,
and more still have the grounds to claim that right. And
most importantly there must be many speakers because each

one has something *different* to say. I am tempted to aver that
the 'specificity' of Europe is somehow related to that multiplicity and variety of speakers. Europe is the pluralist culture
avant le lettre. In that lay its strength, and perhaps even its
uniqueness. The 'melting pot' idea was not born in Europe.
We, 'the Europeans', have been brought up among variety
and spend our lives in the company of difference. We have
slowly learnt the difficult art of living with difference *peace-
fully*, but we had to learn. It is sometimes said that the
inherent 'universalism' of the European spirit consists in its
ability to converse with what is foreign to it. But we may
say that Europe could be seen as a greenhouse of universal
humanity because of its own amazing aptitude for com-
municating across the cultural (or any other) divides. This is
infinitely more important – seminal, promising – than unam-
biguous 'identity'. Before you may recognize the Other as a
problem deserving respectful attention, you must first question yourself and recognize your own ambiguity. *Pensée
unique* is the most sinister enemy of universality. For most
of its history Europe was on the way to elsewhere. And
travellers tend to be vigilant.

Do I fit into this setting? I would strongly wish to. I hope
I do. But one thing I can honestly say is that I have tried to,
as hard as I can.

*Does it follow that there is a kind of 'elective affinity' between
European culture and critical theory?*

Santayana described culture – all culture, any culture – as a
'knife pressed against the future'. Culture is about making
things different from what they are; the future different
from the present. And that cutting into things, making them
different from what they are and what they would be if no
knife were applied, is not a one-off act, though each time
the knife is applied the intention may be to make *this* cutting
the last. Pierre Boulez said that arts struggle to transform
the improbable into the inevitable. I believe that this is
precisely what 'culture does' and what, intuitively, sets the

imagery of culture apart from that of the 'structure'. Structures emerge at the far end of culture's struggle. They stand for the 'inevitable', only to be eroded and in the end folded up, cut into pieces and dissolved by the culture's indefatigable and intransigent rebelliousness, pugnacity and swagger. Culture is a *permanent revolution* of sorts. To say 'culture' is to make another attempt to account for the fact that the human world (the world moulded by the humans and the world which moulds the humans) is perpetually, unavoidably and unremediably *noch nicht geworden* (not-yet-accomplished), as Ernst Bloch beautifully put it.

I am aware that this is not the use of the term 'culture' that is universally accepted. Quite the contrary: all too often 'culture' (particularly in its classical anthropological uses) stood for a *soi-distant* service station of structure, an instrument of continuity, reproduction of sameness and resistance to change. I first heard of culture in the context of the 'modernization' theories which were fashionable in my youth. In that context, 'culture' was a kind of residual notion, something akin to a virus or 'bug', a name for the baffling resistance which confounds the theoretical predictions and the persistence of differences which theory, aimed at modelling development understood as following a preordained trajectory of 'maturation', could not explain and whose causes it was unable to locate without undermining its own foundations. 'Culture' in that context stood for inertia, not movement and change, and was practically synonymous with 'habit', 'routine', absence of reflection, bias, prejudice. Culture was what made people willingly do what they must do (that was called 'ethos', 'values' or 'standards' – cognitive or cathectic), or rendered their actions regular independently of their will (that was called 'learning' or 'acculturation'). Such a view of culture as a 'preservative', as a stabilizing and conserving substance, is very much alive in the 'multiculturalism' ideologies which are presently fashionable. Only the attached sign has changed, from negative to positive, as the universalizing ambition has been taken away from the refurbished vision of 'progress'.

If, however, we agree to use the concept of culture in the
way here suggested, then theory which takes culture
seriously, as the specifically human mode of being, cannot
but be a 'critical' theory. By that last term I do not understand any specific school. 'Critical theory' could be set aside
and put in a separate file of 'a school' only if or when
mainstream sociology was busy modelling the reproduction
of sameness and reaffirming the essential monotoneity of
societal (systemic) self-reproduction. What I understand by
that term is the kind of theorizing which accepts that, first,
'things are not necessarily what they seem to be', and
second, that 'the world may be different from what it is'. A
kind of theorizing, in other words, which spells out *explicitly*
what the nature of the cultural mode-of-being assumes
implicitly. Once you accept culture with its endemic restlessness and its inborn inclination to transcendence as the foun-
dational characteristic of the human mode-of-being, the idea
of 'critical theory' appears pleonastic, like 'buttery butter' or
'metallic iron'. Theory which wants to be faithful and
adequate to its object cannot but be 'critical'.

What follows is that I do not consider 'critical theory' to
be a badge of school membership (unless you take 'critical
theory' to be an event in history and associate that concept
with a fully defined group of people like the founders and
members of the Frankfurt Institute, and others who trace
their pedigree to that institution). It does not set apart a
distinct body of knowledge. You can hardly follow a sociological vocation while embracing a Panglossian view of the
world. If this is the case, then being a critical theorist does
not determine the substance of your theory. Substantially,
critical theories may and do differ widely. What unites them
is a similar treatment of the sociological vocation; a concern
with keeping the forever inexhausted and unfulfilled human
potential open, fighting back all attempts to foreclose and
pre-empt the further unravelling of human possibilities,
prodding human society to go on questioning itself and
preventing that questioning from ever stalling or being
declared finished. In short, it is not just that it is possible to

be a critical theorist while holding widely different views than other critical theorists. I believe that substantive variety, uncovering the plurality of possibilities and their 'undecided' status, is a *conditio sine qua non*, and hopefully also the permanent condition, of sociology capable of performing its critical destiny.

And as time goes by, changing the focus and the substantive proposition is inevitable, if the critical knife pressed against the future is to stay sharp. The dangers threatening human possibilities change, as well as the distribution of 'blind spots' in human experience which make the stifling of possibilities effective. In *Liquid Modernity* I tried to sketch the most crucial of such changes which render urgent the rethinking of the target and the strategy of critical thought.

To sum up: critical theory? Sociology as the activity of social critique? Business as usual. But the raw stuff has changed, and the profile of demand, and so the nature of the product. And as always, the question of management has not been decided and is unlikely to be decided in the foreseeable future.

It would probably be helpful to bring the discussion down to earth a little more and ask you to situate your work in the context of some of the other leading social thinkers of the present. In terms of range, scope and concerns you deal with themes and issues which resonate with the interests which can be found most obviously in the work of writers such as Foucault, Bourdieu and Elias. What is your affinity with the work of these, or indeed other, thinkers?

Affinity, as you know, tends to be selective (by the way, another pleonasm born of incorrect translation of Weber: the German language has no separate word for 'affinity' and calls it *Wahlverwandschaft*, which means 'selected kinship': you do not select your kin, but affinity is by definition selective). Intellectual affinity tends to be selective in a multiple sense. First the author chooses his inspirations, then readers spot similarities which might have been, but need not be, noted by the author. Then others, writers or readers, find the author's story resonant with their own articulated or intuitive views and, so to speak, volunteer their affinity. Which sort of affinities do you wish me to speak about? For obvious reasons, I am competent, if at all, to pronounce only on the first.

Affinities of that first kind are too many to be listed in full. In a short list, I would include, off-the-cuff: Richard Sennett, Richard Rorty, Anthony Giddens, Claus Offe, Pierre Bourdieu, Ulrich Beck, Claude Lévi-Strauss, Loïc Wacquant, Michel Maffesoli, Odo Marquard, Nils Christie, Henning Bech, Alberto Melucci, to name but a few of those who go on writing and supplying me with new ideas. Even that list is far from full. I am in debt to many more writers. I am fully aware of the debts and I would never risk making their inventory if not pressed by you. My affinities, to be sure, are selective in a double sense: I select the writers, but also in their writings I select (or rather: it 'selects itself' in the course of reading) what fits my current concerns most directly. I have chosen them however as my spiritual kith and kin because invariably, whenever reading their work, I have the feeling of shared concerns and purposes. All too often they articulate for me the ideas which rattled below the level of consciousness, pushing to be released, or which I myself was inept in naming or expressing clearly. Some other times they open new vistas which I did not suspect, or of whose significance I was not aware. Each time, though, I feel that we are 'in the same business', and that I've been trying, with mixed success, to broadcast on the same wavelength as they.

'Affinities' would not be properly acknowledged if sources of inspiration of another kind were not mentioned. There are authors to whom I owe my essential cognitive frames. Prime place among them belongs to Mary Douglas and Michel Crozier. To Douglas I owe my understanding of the social production and effects of ambivalence; to Crozier, the comprehension of uncertainty as the stake in the power game. As you have probably noticed, both ideas keep cropping up incessantly in virtually every analytical attempt I make, many years after I read *Purity and Danger* and *The Bureaucratic Phenomenon*. Affinities cannot be measured by the number of references. The most important ones do not need footnotes.

You rate Castoriadis very highly indeed. What inspiration do you take from his work?

I am glad that you've mentioned Castoriadis. He has occupied a special place among my selected kinspeople since I was struck by the parallelity *(toutes proportions gardées!)* of our life itineraries, of the similarity of that curious and difficult to disentangle mixture of continuity and discontinuity. In the year of Castoriadis's death I attempted to spell out the reasons why I feel so uncannily close to his experience. Let me quote from an unpublished (and unfinished) text:

> If, as Heidegger suggested, life is a process of perpetual recapitulation and reabsorption, each successive recapitulation of the individual life is inevitably carried out in changed circumstances and within changed cognitive frames: not everything in the past life is amenable to recapitulation and absorption, at least not without profound change of form. For most carriers of water and hewers of wood this remains a private worry, the question of settling accounts in secret or going on living with the accounts unsettled. Privacy is not an option, however, for the writers of books and actors of public space. Those among them who had the mixed blessing to be seen as *living long* (and with generations treading on each other's heels, few have that blessing denied) often find themselves pushed or tempted to spend a later part of their life criticizing its earlier parts, rewriting their own books and redoing their own deeds: trying to make sense of what seemed to have sense once but has lost it, fighting once more the long forgotten battles, seeking admission to the chorus of detractors of the experience which shaped their generation and of the strategies they chose to respond to it. The Ph.D.

students face a daunting task when struggling to tie together the writings produced in successive decades of 'the same' author's life and to concoct a sense joint to them all, or at least to conjure up an inkling of a straight line in the author's intellectual meanders. There are but few prominent exceptions to that rule – and Cornelius Castoriadis is most remarkable among them. At no stage of his long creative life stood Castoriadis (a member of the Greek Resistance who, like Kostas Axelos and Kostas Papaioannou joined the ranks of French intellectuals in 1940s) aloof: at no stage did he attempt to steer clear from the concerns, worries and ambitions of his contemporaries: never did he seek to locate his own interests at a safe distance from the main intellectual battlegrounds of the time. Castoriadis's life came close to that ideal of weaving together biography with history, which many dream of, many more pay lip-service to, but only a few truly manage to implement in their lives.

The assembly of his works reads like an intellectual chronicle of the age, a faithful record of successive generations' experiences, discoveries and blind spots, hopes and disappointments, naivetés and wisdoms. Castoriadis never took that lofty and arrogant posture of a supposedly 'objective observer', who claims to be sitting on a perch from which the daily exertions of the ordinary folk may be contemplated in all their narrow-mindedness and short-sightedness, censured, and if need be derided. He shared in those exertions, never far from the front-line. And yet there is a striking continuity, consistency, cohesion and unity of purpose as well as an unswerving loyalty to the lifelong project, in Castoriadis's *oeuvre* stretched over fifty years and several generations.

There is a sovereign purpose, guiding idea and a strategic principle in all Castoriadis's works – from the earliest and up to the most recent.

First – the purpose: the stubborn pursuit, be what may, with the help of or despite the twists of history, of the ambitious Enlightenment intention 'to lead a human being to reason'.

Second – the ideal that is needed to achieve this purpose (if its achievement is at all possible) is that a human being's 'adherence to a heteronomous institution of society,

his internalization of the representations in which the institution is embodied, ceases'. That autonomy which could be
reached solely through the self-emancipation from' the
incurably heteronomous institutions is – Castoriadis never
stops repeating – both made possible by our modern society
and actively hampered by it: this society assures that the
possibility is real, but in no way guarantees that it will ever
become a reality. There are in modern society the institutional *conditions* of autonomy – but no institutional foundations: '*the value of our tradition is that it has also created* the
project of autonomy, democracy and philosophy, and also
that it has created, and given value to, the possibility of *choice*
(impossible, for example, for true Jews, Christians, or
Muslims).'

Third – the strategic principle, which shows itself to be an
ethical principle through and through: 'what we have to do
is face up to our tragic condition – which is what post-
Hellenic ethics, since Plato, have tried to occult: human life
ought to be posited as an absolute, but it cannot always be
so. People clearly don't like that. They have transferred the
Hebraic and Christian Promise onto the requirement for a
"rational foundation" and the Decalogue onto the demand for
a book of ethical recipes or for a "rule" that would give in
advance the answer to all cases that might present themselves. Fear of freedom, desperate need for assurance, occul-
tation of our tragic condition.'

And so, when faithful to the purpose and armed with the
idea how the cause of that purpose could be best served, we
are left with a precept which is fairly straightforward,
though not for that reason easy to follow: '"Become autonomous" and "contribute as much as you can to others'
becoming autonomous". This precept is not easy to
implement – since the "tragic condition" of humanity is precisely the fact that "no problem is resolved in advance. We
have to create the good, under imperfectly known and
uncertain conditions. The project of autonomy is end and
guide, it does not resolve for us effectively actual situations."
And so the "imperfect knowledge" and "uncertainty of conditions" as well as the uncertainty of outcomes are likely to
accompany our efforts "to create the good" as long as those
efforts would last.'

The purpose, the idea and the strategic principle unite Castoriadis's work over many years, which began with the heady days of *Socialisme ou Barbarie* and continued in the office of a practising psychoanalyst and the study-room of the retired economist of the OECD. There were shifts of attention and political foci of inquiry – but each move was inspired by the intention of finding the right territory where the purpose stood a better chance of being fulfilled, the idea could be better accommodated and the principle deployed to a better effect.

In your view what is the relationship of sociology to other academic disciplines?

This is a hardy perennial of a question. I also suspect that it is a red herring. For reasons which can be as easily understood as they are unconvincing, it crops up in every introductory course offered to first-year sociology students. This is understandable, since academe is a world of cut-throat competition for funds, and some people need to prove that there are kinds of research and expertise which only they can deliver, and since the world outside the academe is similar so the credentials which students come to collect and take with them on leaving must bear names which make the competences of their holders eligible and so sellable. But this is also unconvincing, since there is little substance to the academic divisions apart from such necessities as arise from a mixture of bureaucratic and market considerations. And I suppose that the hotter the debate about the disciplinary boundaries and permissible/illegal border traffic, the less 'natural' the frontiers must be and the more artificial and arbitrary the lines drawn.

Émile Durkheim and his contemporaries had to attach a lot of attention to the question of the uniqueness of sociology and its relation to 'older' branches of scholarship (that is, to disciplines academically established and no longer considered as illegitimate immigrants *sans papiers*). For them, mustering the best arguments they could to prove their right to separate chairs was indeed a matter of life and death. Since then, we go on arguing by inertia rather than necessity, still following one of the two strategies; seeking like Durkheim a separate realm of 'facts' which others leave fallow, or insisting like Weber on the uniqueness of the way of their processing. The time dedicated to argumentation could however be spent better, since sociology is 'reality' not a 'proposition'. It long ago acquired academic passports and its continuous reproduction is secure, having become a matter of institutional logic.

Whatever the spokesmen for sociology may say about the nature of their work, sociology is an ongoing dialogue with human experience, and that experience, unlike the university buildings, is not divided into departments, let alone tightly sealed departments. Academics may refuse or neglect to read their next floor neighbour's work and so carry unscathed the conviction of their own separate identity, but this cannot be said of human experience, in which the sociological, the political, the economic, the philosophical, the psychological, the historical, the poetic and what not are blended to the extent that no single ingredient can salvage its substance or identity in case of separation. I would go as far as to say that however hard it may try, sociology would never win the 'war of independence'. More to the point, it would never survive a victorious outcome of such a war, were it at all conceivable. The discursive formation bearing the name of sociology is porous on all sides and is notorious for its enormous, insatiable absorptive power. Personally, I believe that this is sociology's strength, not weakness. I believe that the future of sociology is assured precisely because it comes nearer than any other academic discipline to embracing human experience in its entirety.

So let us leave the foreign policy and diplomacy worries aside and return to the tasks that really matter.

Following on from the last question about the place and nature of sociology, would you agree with the claim which is often made nowadays that we live in a totally different world from that which was inhabited by the founders of sociology and that we must therefore consign Marx, Durkheim, Weber to the dustbin and begin afresh?

I've lived long, perhaps too long to take such claims seriously. I've learned that nothing is truly new and unprecedented, and that nothing disappears without trace. In our times waste is the most thriving and most rapidly growing industry sector. We also live among the cavalcade of celebrities and fashion. And so it may seem credible that 'from dustbin thou arose and to dustbin thou shalt return.' This is, though, one of those self-deceptions which sociology is bound to pierce if it is to open the truth of the human condition to the users' scrutiny. The reality of any 'use-by date' is the withdrawal of the product from supermarket shelves; the sole reality of Marx, Weber or Durkheim becoming 'outdated' is to stop reading them. We tend to move from hype to hype and books seldom survive the few-days-long headlines season. This 'instant obsolescence' of commodities on promotion is, though, a ripple on the surface of culture's deep waters, and judging the deep currents by surface wrinkles would be an error no serious navigator would commit. Pitirim Sorokin once coined the phrase 'Columbus complex' for 'getting bored with issues before they are solved', a habit which Gordon Allport picked up as the most odious of academic maladies. Sorokin suggested that the most commonly used shortcut to the 'Columbus complex' is ignorance.

I believe that instant obsolescence-cum-forgetting is an indispensable factor of the economy of waste, and so I suspect that the proclamations of the 'end' of this or that, whether of history or of the founding stones of sociology, will go on being made regardless of their inanity. But who, if not us – the sociologists – should know better? There is no present except the continuous recapitulation of the past. Milan Kundera wrote that the beauty of the episode is that it has a clear-cut end, but the nastiness of the episode is that you never know whether it was indeed but an episode.

There is no Devil's Island or high-tech security prison from which the exiled cannot return to haunt us.

In order to pull this conversation to an end, could you summarize your concerns in a paragraph?

I can try to answer the question in a book or in a sentence, hardly in a paragraph (one needs the *Guardian Editor* editor's talent to do the latter; but then books selected for summarizing in *The Editor* as a rule are such as cannot lose much in the process of squeezing).[2]

So, a sentence. Not mine – Albert Camus's:

> there is beauty and there are the humiliated. Whatever difficulties the enterprise may present, I should like never to be unfaithful either to the second or the first.

Conversation 2

Ethics and Human Values

KEITH TESTER *At the end of the last conversation you took up Camus's dictum about not wanting to be unfaithful either to beauty or humiliation as something like the motif for your own social thought. It is perfectly clear from your adoption of Camus, as indeed from nearly every page of your own work, that your work is ethical in its very nature and that it drips with ethical commitment.*

Can you address this issue as a starting point for this discussion? There is the large question: why ought social thought to be ethical? And then there is the relatively more local question: why is your own work so ethically committed? Indeed, what is ethics?

ZYGMUNT BAUMAN Time and again I read in the reviews of my books that I am a follower of Rousseau: Bauman, some reviewers say, assumes that humans are intrinsically good, and that being evil is an extraordinary, abnormal condition of a social, rather than an individual, provenance. This has never been my view, though. It could not be, as I'd find it exceedingly difficult, nay impossible, to think of the 'human person' outside of society or of 'society' independently of the individuals who compose it. If humans are something 'intrinsically', they are *social*.

It is a common enough question: are humans 'by nature' good, as Jean-Jacques insisted, or are they 'by nature' evil, as Hobbes assumed? My answer to this question would be:

neither, and we would not know it if they were. What we may reasonably suppose, though, is that humans are, 'by nature', *moral* and that being moral is perhaps the constitutive attribute of humanity, a feature that makes the human condition unique and sets it apart from any other modes of being-in-the-world. The very fact that the question about the goodness or evil of human nature is asked (that it *can* be asked) is all the proof we need that this is the case.

'Being moral' does not, necessarily, mean 'being good'. But it does mean having eaten from the tree of knowledge of good and evil and knowing that things and acts may be good or evil. Well, in order to know that, humans need another, preliminary, awareness: that things and deeds may be different than they are. One could muse that this has something to do with the particle 'no' which all languages that humans deploy to recast the world out there in the *Lebenswelt*, existence into experience, contain. 'No' would make no sense unless it was assumed that one can act in more than one way, or that affairs 'out there' could be arranged in more than one way. 'No' implies that things *do not have to be as they currently are*, that they can be altered: also made better than they currently are. If it were not for that, all talk about 'morality' would be empty. As a matter of fact, there would be no talk about morality: morality, after all (perhaps rather *first of all*) is about *choice*. No choice, no morality. 'The mountain is cold, but it isn't wicked. The winds knock down trees, but they aren't evil' – as Aharon Appelfeld, one of the great moral story-tellers of our time, put it.

On that primary condition of knowing that things could be different from what they are, there are many glosses, divine and secular, civic or hedonistic. But they all accompany (justify and sustain) an effort to give some alternatives preference over others. That effort I call 'ethics': a project to give certain occurrences a higher degree of probability than they otherwise would have, and to reduce the probability of their alternatives to a minimum, or to eliminate their possibility altogether. This is what 'society' is about. Society is an ongoing effort to *structure* – and structure is nothing but a likelihood of 'order': the manipulation of probabilities, making the improbable or uncertain inevitable, into a rule, into a regular, repetitive event. 'Culture' we call a similar effort to reduce the randomness of human conduct, to force that conduct to abide by a pattern. All in all, culture is about putting some kinds of choices above all the others.

All that – society, social order, culture – would be inconceivable if morality were not the primary predicament of humans: even if, paradoxically, they are all attempts to render that predicament irrelevant and 'neutralize' its consequences. I am tempted to say that society is a contraption helping humans to cope with the fate of being moral beings, that fate being the necessity of making choices with the knowledge (or at least a suspicion in case efforts are made to suppress or deny that knowledge) that they are but choices. Society engraves the pattern of ethics upon the raw and pliable stuff of morality. Ethics is a social product because morality is not. And if sociology is a study of society, it is and cannot but be, knowingly or not, an inquiry into the ways in which ethical rules are constructed and 'made to stick', ways in which choices are made by humans and for the humans, alternative possibilities promoted, stifled and otherwise manipulated.

If this is what sociology is doomed to do, then the 'ethical neutrality' often demanded of sociologists is either hypocrisy or self-delusion. Societies are 'coordinated choices', and any society you study is one reality among many, one choice among many. Like all choices, that society may be good or bad, but in each case it may be made better than it is. Getting this particular fact straight is already a moral act, committed by the moral beings who happen to be sociologists (let me note that this circumstance makes sociologists, however hard they try to prove their loyalty, seem suspicious to the powers-that-be who would rather have people believe that 'there is no alternative' and that choices are not really choices). What follows after that is making another choice between good and evil that a moral being cannot but go on making. One can side with the selection made by the society one describes from inside, one can even take a Panglossian view of 'this being the best of possible worlds', and proceed to lubricate the wheels of the social mechanism which makes the selection stick. Or one can question the wisdom of the selection, insist on counting its costs, calculate the volume of human distress that could be avoided were the selection altered.

Being moral means knowing that things may be good or bad. But it does not mean knowing, let alone knowing for sure, *which* things are good and *which* are bad. Being moral means being bound to make choices under conditions of acute and painful uncertainty. I guess that what we know more clearly (though we would be hard put when asked to argue our case) is what is evil. Of that, we have on the whole little doubt: we are shocked and mortified, we feel disgusted, appalled, repelled. The 'good' is, in the language of semiotics, the marked member of the opposition. The image of the good comes later, with a 'negative sign', as a rectification of evil. But apart from the hope that the evil or part of it will go away, we are not sure that whatever comes in its place will be good. I suppose that seldom, if ever, do we find that replacement 'good enough', since in every situation, also in the new one, we keep facing the same dilemma between good and evil. Moral life, the life of choice between good and evil, is therefore filled with the anxiety of self-reprobation and self-recrimination. To be moral means never to feel *good enough*: that feeling, I am inclined to believe, stands behind the endemic urge to transcendence and accounts for the notorious human restlessness regarding everything human. But it also generates a lot of unhappiness and a constant doubt that poisons even the greatest of self-satisfactions. This is when ethics comes in handy; as a tranquillizer, a medicine to put qualms to rest, a drug to mitigate pangs of conscience. As with all medicines, though, it is far from foolproof. In the long run, if taken daily, it may prompt an 'iatrogenic' disease, destroy the organism's immunity system, and deprive the self of the little ability it might have had of facing up to moral dilemmas and going after the good on its own.

My wise friend Leszek Kolakowski once wrote an essay 'In Praise of Inconsistency'. He also wrote another essay called 'Ethics without a Code' (in my vocabulary, the title would be 'Morality without Ethics'). I think the two phrases are closely related. An alternative to the strict, precise and above all binding (perhaps even authoritarian) ethical code is a life of vacillation. The restless and indefatigable search for the ways to do away with evil can hardly run in a straight line, since the steps which are hoped to be good as a rule bring new evils, and on a closer examination do not appear to be as good as hoped. I think that the human itinerary (individual as much as collective, biographical as much as historical) is pendulum-like rather than drawn with a ruler. For beings cast in a moral situation, the rule-supported consistency is not necessarily a virtue. For the humans who have eaten from the tree of knowledge of good and evil (a feast that offers a reliable knowledge of evil but a rather misty idea of good) it is, it seems to me, an impossibility.

And so there is humiliation, that ugliness of being that repels us, and there is (should be, must be) beauty, that projected goodness to which, repelled, we run for shelter. We cannot be faithful to the humiliated unless we reach for beauty. Running away from, projected as running towards. In my reading, Camus restates Walter Benjamin's decoding of 'progress'. Like history, we the moral selves move with our backs turned towards the future, pushed back-to-front by the horrors of the past. The future no sooner comes in for scrutiny than it becomes in its turn a past and its ugliness shows.

I am so pleased that you see my work as 'dripping with ethical commitment'. This is how I would like it to be, though as a moral person I do not dare to say that it indeed is, or is *sufficiently*. But I suspect that it would be saturated with ethics whether or not this were my conscious wish. I do not believe that a student of human reality may be ethically *neutral*. The sole choice we face is one between loyalty to the humiliated and to beauty, and indifference to both. It is like any other choice a moral being confronts: between taking and refusing to take responsibility for one's responsibility.

The ethical aspect has been a constant characteristic of your work. In the last conversation you alluded to socialism in a way which implies that you saw it very much as an ethical ambition rather than as a principle of social engineering or institutional change. Such a theme is implicit in one of your first 'English period' books, Socialism: The Active Utopia. *What does it mean to describe socialism as a utopia? Does utopia represent a flight of human ambition and is it in that way that socialism could be seen as ethical?*

I suspect that in our social-scientific usage all too often we unduly narrow down the concept of 'utopia' to the early-modern blueprints of the good society, understood as a kind of totality which pre-empts its members' choices and determines in advance their goodness, however understood. A kind of totality in which, purely and simply, 'being evil' would be an impossibility. One of the first pronouncements of the modern spirit was Alberti's idea of perfection as a state of affairs in which any change could only be a change for the worse. This is, I admit, an attractive and alluring prospect (even if it was long suspected that paradise's affliction would be the boredom emanating from purposelessness of being). The idea of once and for all getting rid of the torments of choice and uncertainty cannot but allure the tormented.

Such peculiar utopias reflected the ambitions, and the self-delusions, of the modern spirit. Let us use our power of choice to put an end to the trials and tribulations of choice. Let us put an end to contingency, ambivalence, ignorance, blunders: there is an end to the road, a point of arrival where the travellers may rest and enjoy the fruits of their travel. I suppose that much of all that was present in my fascination with the bold socialist project. So there was, I am afraid, an immoderate measure of 'social engineering' in the project I adored, an idea of change in order to end the need to change. However, an idea of 'historical inevitability' was at no time, and most certainly not after my encounter with Gramsci, part of my understanding of socialism as 'good society'. At the time that I wrote *Socialism: The Active Utopia*, something had broken once for all: the vision of socialism (or, for that matter, of the 'good society') as a state to be achieved, a state bound to become at some point 'the final state' of humanity. Instead, there emerged the vision of socialism (and more generally of utopia) as a horizon, constantly on the move, perpetually receding, but guiding the travel; or like a spike prodding the conscience, a nagging rebuke that cast complacency and self-adoration out of bounds and out of question. It was now the utopia itself, not the state of affairs it was meant to bring about, that bore the mark of eternity. Its attraction was not in the promise of rest, but in keeping humans forever on the move, in calling them to fight ever new injustices and to take the side of the successive echelons of the left behind, injured, humiliated.

I am now inclined to accept that utopia is an undetachable part of the human condition, just like morality. I owe that view to Ernst Bloch. I remember being deeply impressed by his definition of human being as 'intention pointing ahead', and of 'human nature' as 'something which still must be found'. I was impressed by his propositions that the sole 'being' possible for the moment – for any moment – is 'being before itself', and that 'in both man and the world the essential thing is still outstanding, waiting, in fear of coming to naught, in hope of succeeding', and that the world is a 'vast encounter full of future'. The 'human essence' lying forever in the future, the pool of human possibilities remaining forever unexhausted, and the future itself being unknown and unknowable, impossible to adumbrate ('the absolute other', in Levinas's vocabulary). Such a view of human modality breathes tolerance, offers the benefit of the doubt, teaches modesty and self-restraint. If you know exactly what the *good society* is like, any cruelty you commit in its name is justified and absolved. But we can be *good to each other* and abstain from cruelty only when we are unsure of our wisdom and admit a possibility of error. This is a banal truth once it has been stated, and yet it needs repeating since it is so seldom practised. I would count Bloch among the most powerful ethical thinkers of the past century, alongside Levinas, Løgstrup, Jonas.

I now believe that utopia is one of humanity's constituents, a 'constant' in the human way of being-in-the-world. This does not mean that all utopias are equally good. Utopias may lead to a better life as much as they may mislead and turn away from what a better life would require to be done. The 'deregulated' and 'privatized' utopias of our individualized world I assign to the latter category.

Is this utopian aspect also the basis of your understanding of the value of culture? In Culture as Praxis, *you tie culture to human ambition, creation and, in all, to freedom from necessity and compulsion. This is also the nub of your comments about 'human values' in your inaugural lecture at the University of Leeds in 1971.*

Yes, it is my conviction that morality and culture are *cancellations of necessity* (even if the ostensible purpose of culture tends to be to conjure up necessity out of contingency, determination out of randomness). And it is my conviction that freedom is the 'natural condition' of humanity (even if most of humanity's history has been dedicated to using that freedom to cancel free choice). It is also my conviction that this rising above necessity which is called freedom is the secret of the amazing creativity which humans go on demonstrating when it comes to seeking and finding and inventing the modes of being-in-the-world.

Unfreedom is not on the cards, though not for the lack of trying. One thing which humans with all their freedom cannot accomplish is to stop being free: underdetermined, unfinished, incomplete, 'still outstanding'. There is always something left to do, a business to finish, a stretch of the road to pass. In this respect, social settings do not differ much from each other. Where they do differ is the degree to which that 'something to do' is prescribed and thereafter channelled into patterns. But even if the task is to follow a pattern and a routine, to *conform* to standards made obligatory, the requisite of 'conformity' would make little sense if there were not the possibility *not to conform*, go a different way, pursue alternative ways, whether tacitly or overtly recognized. Freedom is the uppermost among human values. But first and foremost it is a *fate*. Free beings, since they are free, may embrace that fate or try to escape from it, make it into their vocation or fight against it: this is also the capacity which they owe to their freedom. If freedom is a value, it is also an utterly ambivalent one. It attracts and repels at the same time. Erich Fromm wrote of the escape from freedom as one of the most common motives of human endeavours, while Alfred Schütz pointed to our equally common inclination to hide 'in-order-to' motives behind 'because-of' motives. It is somehow less unnerving, disconcerting and frightening to account for one's action using the terms 'I had to' rather than 'I wanted'. Hence the treacherous allure of 'there is no alternative' and 'one way only' ideologies, as well as the awesome seductive power of totalitarian baits. So many of us, so often, feel that they would be glad if their freedom were denied, contested or taken away. And there is never a shortage of offers to do just that. Being free calls for a cool head and steely nerves.

In our time of 'liquid modernity' there is more reason than at any other time for a 'vertigo of freedom'. Standards to which one could conform are notorious for being melted as soon as they are moulded, routines in which one could hide from choice change too quickly for sedimenting into habits, 'disembedding' goes forth unabated. But all too often and for too many there are only motel beds and sleeping bags available for re-embedding. Truthfully or not, we are told daily that possibilities are unlimited and that it is up to us to pick and choose those that fit us best; more importantly, we are punished for failing to find them, as if what we had been told of their availability were true. We have come dangerously close to Samuel Butler's *Erewhon*, where speculators and embezzlers were treated as victims of distress, were pitied and tenderly cared for and bathed in public sympathy, while the poor and the sick were seen as criminals and imprisoned; where 'luck was the only fit object of human veneration', where it was recognized that 'how far a man has any right to be more lucky and hence more venerable than his neighbours is a point that always has been, and always will be, settled proximately by the kind of higgling and haggling of the market, and ultimately by brute force', and where a judge replied to the unlucky people's plea for mercy with 'you may say that it is your misfortune to be criminal: I answer that it is your crime to be unfortunate.'

The present-day rendition of the eternal 'there is no alternative' expedient is also novel. What is insinuated now is that there is no alternative to the assumption that the volume of alternatives 'within everybody's reach' is infinite; and to society being run and its members treated as if that assumption were true. The assumption is not true, however, and cannot become true as long as the present-day decoupling of freedom and security, the two values which cannot be entertained in separation, persists. We are called to believe today that security is disempowering, disabling, breeding the resented 'dependency' and altogether constraining the human agents' freedom. What is passed over in silence is that acrobatics and rope-walking without a safety net are an art few people can master and a recipe for disaster for all the rest. Take away security, and freedom is the first casualty.

Modernity and the Holocaust can be seen, with all the insight of retrospective wisdom, as a turning point in your thought. This is the book in which Levinas appears in your work. Could you say something about why you turned to Levinas and his ethic of care for the Other?

What had happened, it seems, to my thinking between *Socialism: The Active Utopia* and *Modernity and the Holocaust* was that the perspective from which I viewed beauty and humiliation and ugliness widened. Gradually, the victims of economic injustice began to appear to me as a particular case of a much wider, more ubiquitous and stubborn phenomenon of the 'stranger'. I began to see deprivation as an artifact of exclusion rather than its prime cause, and the plight of industrial workers which prompted socialist utopia in its 'counterculture of capitalism' form as a peculiar, and historically limited, form of the social production of outcasts. Norbert Elias arrived there first (in his *Established and Outsiders*), but I guess that what set me on that line of thinking was Mary Douglas's *Purity and Danger*. It took some time for that inspiration to sink in and even longer to take root and give fruit: to realize that most if not all of the forbidding nastiness of human degradation and socially produced indignity is the by-product of the search for order and fear of disturbance, brought to its radical, obsessive extreme by modernity, itself a desperate response to the collapse of the self-reproducing order of the *ancien régime*. I suppose that when writing *Socialism: The Active Utopia* I came to the threshold of that realization: it shows in the premonition that what the socialist utopia needed was to redeploy itself as a 'counterculture of *modernity*'. But it took a few more years to think through the consequences.

During thinking through and writing up *Modernity and the Holocaust*, Levinas came as an afterthought; also as a last straw. There was Nechama Tec's discovery that those who were shocked by the sight of suffering deeply enough to swim against the tide and risk all to help the sufferers came from all of the 'social categories' which, according to the sociological creed, determine the ethicality of human conduct. Clearly then, moral acts meant *breaching* rather than *following* the socially designed and monitored norms. And there was Hannah Arendt's observation that those who managed to break out from the genocidal orgy had to stand up against the dominant standards of their society and could not count on any support from socially imposed norms and official ethical precepts, and that the ability to go against one's society could be a prerequisite of a moral act. Both Tec's findings and Arendt's observation were amply corroborated by the failure of all of the ostensible 'guardian institutions of morality' to arrest, let alone prevent, the death industry from doing its job. That cast a huge doubt on the canonical, Durkheimian, view of morality as the product of society and the achievement of sanction-assisted social control. This was a view which I treated with a good deal of suspicion anyway on account of its ethical indifference: if there is nothing to the morality of the members of society but the will of the society to which they belong, on what ground could one dispute the morality of any norm? And where could one find a springboard for resisting an evil norm? If there is nothing morality can count on except societally authored precepts and societally administered sanctions, its chances are, to say the least, slim, and its future precarious.

But if Durkheim's hallowed, almost universally accepted and seldom questioned version of morality is faulty, what can we put in its place? Whatever we do put in its place must take into account the presence of societies which, far from preventing cruelty, may actually endorse and promote it. It must accept that what societies do is *manipulate* morality rather than *produce* it. And it must anchor morality and the moral self in a ground more solid and reliable than the notoriously protean and whimsical 'majority opinions' and their institutional armouries. This was the big question mark that emerged during my study of the lessons of the Holocaust, and Levinas came as the God-sent answer. I distinctly remember the 'eureka!', the 'this is it!' feeling when reading that 'ethics comes before ontology.'

I've found two messages in that statement. First (since in a world with ethics but without ontology there is no 'before' or 'later', but only 'better' and 'worse'), that it is the socially produced reality which needs to justify itself, tried and judged at the tribunal of ethics, instead of usurping the right to decide what is and what is not moral. Second, that either sources of morality can be found in a modality of human existence which is immune to the vagaries of social arrangements, or they are, purely and simply, non-existent. Morality cannot be 'made' like other human institutions. Rather it is the stuff in which human arrangements are carved. It is their, to deploy Aristotle's terminology, 'material cause'. And so the too often forgotten or dismissed, but indispensable condition of the very possibility of carving them. Morality *is*; it neither can nor needs to give its reasons nor must it prove its rights. The question 'why should I be moral?' is the end, not the beginning of morality; a suspicious question as much as it is obtrusive and ubiquitous in a society that tends to expropriate the moral self from its responsibility, offering in exchange conformity to a rule.

I knew but a small part of Levinas's writing when the manuscript of *Modernity and the Holocaust* was sent to the printers. I studied it in depth later on, and I learned many other things on top of what found its way into the last chapter of that book. And I came to admire Levinas for other reasons as well, foremost among them the thesis of the inborn ambiguity of the moral condition and the impossibility of 'arguing away' the endemic uncertainty of responsibility. I found in that thesis a glimmer of hope otherwise bereaved in the era of 'liquid modernity' by society shedding all pretensions to its ethical function and gladly ceding the regulation of human intercourse to market forces.

When you turned to Levinas you made a move which is quite contrary to that which was carried out by Hannah Arendt. In her book on Adolf Eichmann, she condemns Eichmann on the grounds that he refused to do his duty as it is established by the categorical imperative. And yet your Holocaust *book can be read as a critique of this kind of analysis; it could be argued that, from a Levinasian point of view, any claims about duty and the like mean putting an abstract ideal in place of the responsibility that the individual has to care for the Other. Could you say something about why you took a path which is quite different to that which Arendt pursued in her condemnation of the Holocaust?*

Here I feel obliged to protest. You imply that the author of *The Origins of Totalitarianism* and *The Human Condition* was a 'strong sociologist' by her frame of mind and temperament if not by her academic appointment, a view alien to the very substance of her work and well-nigh inconceivable in the light of that work. The question asked in *Eichmann in Jerusalem* concerns the sociological problem of the causes of evil, not the philosophical issue of proving that evil is what it is – evil. We could (and would) condemn Eichmann even if Kant had never been born. The big question is why are there Eichmanns who need to be condemned?

My quarrel with Hannah Arendt, if there is any, is not about Kant and the logical consistency or argumentative powers of the categorical imperative. My disagreement concerns her thesis of the 'banality of evil'. Arendt unpacks that baffling phrase as a charge of thoughtlessness: Eichmann was evil *because he did not think*. But it would be a hard task to prove Eichmann's thoughtlessness, unless Arendt uses the term in a different sense than the one commonly accepted and sanctioned by the society we all inhabit. Eichmann was a tremendously successful high-ranking bureaucrat, showered with medals and prizes for the efficiency of his thinking. In applying whatever bureaucracy had defined as logic and rationality, Eichmann was a pastmaster. Had Hitler emerged victorious from the war, universities would compete to have Eichmann among their teachers of managerial science.

I am far from suggesting that thinking is not an important matter and that we can do without it (each act of assuming responsibility for moral responsibility must be a starting point to long and hard thinking). What I do suggest is that Eichmann is not a good example from which to learn the disastrous consequences of the failure to think. Something else, however, can be learned from Eichmann's story: the *rationality* of evil.

Evil, we may learn, could be as impeccably rational as goodness. And correct logical thinking, a thinking abiding by all the rules of rationality, is by itself (that is, unless bridled and guided by moral responsibility) impotent when it comes to stopping evil deeds in their tracks. It may even prove to be evil's most efficient engine.

I also feel uneasy when the problem of evil, an ethical problem through and through, is argued in terms of such morally neutral (indeed, indifferent) terms as 'duty'. There are all sorts of duty, as every army conscript would know, and but few of them are remotely related to the sort of care which we would be willing to define as 'moral'. Was not Eichmann a dutiful person? Was he not always at the beck and call of his superiors, was he not careful not to let down his colleagues-in-crime? There is an unbridgeable abyss separating a duty to the stronger, someone resourceful enough to command, reward and punish, and the duty to the weaker who is not capable of any such things. To avoid this mix-up, which could only further obfuscate the already complex problem, I prefer to speak of the difference between 'responsibility to' (the rules, the rule-makers, the rule-guardians) and the moral responsibility which is always a 'responsibility for' (the well-being and the dignity of the Other). The two responsibilities may work in unison, and lucky is a society in which they do. But their working in concert is by no means their common habit nor a 'natural predilection'.

Modern reason's forte is the power of tools. What counts as the measure of success is efficiency, speed and scale of performance. Its weakness is the vagueness and uncertainty about the ends to which the tools may be applied (as Levinas remarked in his essay on Buber and Marcel, 'intellectual mastery of being proved to be the technological mastery of being as world . . . [T]hough freed by scientific reason, man became the plaything of technological necessities dictating their law to reason.' Levinas notes a growing uncertainty about 'the precise significance of the rational, once wrested free from opinion and ideology'!). Modernity's reason is instrumental; it can say a lot about how things need to be done, but next to nothing about what things ought to be done. Decisions about ends are taken in a way which has little of the 'modern' about it: such decisions are a matter of political and/or military power and ideology. Unlike the efficiency of tools, the propriety of chosen ends cannot be 'proved' or 'disproved': promoting certain ends and stopping other ends from being implemented depend on power struggles, not argument.

Modernity is also about making the world 'clean', 'transparent', predictable and so altogether 'orderly'. Ordering means making reality different than it is, getting rid of the ingredients of reality which are deemed to be responsible for 'impurity', 'opacity', 'contingency' of human condition. Once that road has been entered, one may arrive sooner or later at a verdict that some people be refused help, thrown out or destroyed in the name of a 'greater good' and somebody else's 'greater happiness'. Once you assume that the happy society is a race-clean society, a decision to deport or gas the Jews and the Gypsies is a *rational* way to proceed, and a lot of thinking goes into seeing the job through. Once you assume that the orderly society must be free from dissidents and troublemakers, throwing the heretics in dungeons and shoving the nonconformists out is, again, a rational means to the end.

And so the Holocaust was a legitimate product of modernity. It was, after all, about using the best technology available to cleanse the world of elements which stood in the way of perfection. The model of perfection was in that case a world free of the Jewish 'anti-race' and the casting of the inferior races in the only role that fitted them, servants of the *Herrenrasse*. In other cases of modern genocide, the goals differed. Order could require the extermination of anticommunists and their potential sympathizers (as in Stalin's Russia) or of communists and those suspected of siding with them (as in Argentina or Chile). Or it could require getting rid of people guilty of speaking different tongues or worshipping different gods. Nothing 'modern', let me repeat, about the goals but the self-assured confidence that they could be fulfilled. The grandiosity of the vision and the power of tools matching that grandiosity are thoroughly modern and are unthinkable without modernity. If anything about those genocides could be seen as a *failure* of 'thinking', it is only that most of them stopped short of achieving their purpose. Technology, obviously, was not modern enough.

Doesn't talk in Levinasian terms imply that, without restriction and unfreedom, humans are capable of behaving responsibly towards one another? But, to be a devil's advocate, doesn't history prove that Hobbes was right? Can it not be argued that, left to our own devices, humans are nasty and brutish, our lives violent and short? Can it not be argued that, however violent modernity might have been, things would be much worse if we were left to ourselves?

Neither you nor I have ever met the 'Hobbesian man', a human being cast in a world that does not contain a society, an entity which has already 'prefabricated' the world in which humans carve and mould their *Lebenswelte* by categorizing, classifying, filing, setting apart, selecting the differences that make the difference. I can only repeat after Heidegger that *alles Sein ist 'ursprünglich' Mitsein*. You say 'human' and you imply 'society'. All those facts that 'prove' that 'Hobbes was right', as far as they were 'human facts', had to be societal facts as well. How can we disentangle the 'presocial' from the 'social' here? Did the Croats and the Serbs and the Bosnian Muslims and the Kosovo Albanians who for many years lived next door to each other, travelled in the same trams, worked at the same benches, danced at the same village fêtes and intermarried, suddenly start cutting each other's throats because society had disappeared together with the memory of itself and all the habits it had worked so hard to drill in? Or because other societies took over from the one that fell apart and lost hold? We are never 'left to ourselves' (if there were beings 'left to themselves', they would not be able to know it or articulate their condition anyway). Norman Cohn, the great historian of European cruelty, did not find a single case of a pogrom which was truly spontaneous, that is without organization and plan, without ringleaders, thorough 'ideological mobilization' and a structure of command. No, history does not prove that 'Hobbes was right', and moreover there is no way of ever proving (or for that matter disproving) it.

Furthermore, Levinas's postulate of the pre-ontological

status of ethics is not comparable to Hobbes's fiction of the 'pre-social man', and for that reason it is not in competition with the Hobbesian image. Levinas's thesis is not, like Hobbes's, an *etiological myth*, a story of 'how the state and its authority happened to be born', nor the 'without them a deluge' *plaidoyer* on behalf of the powers that be. Levinas's thesis is a phenomenological proposition, an insight into the sense of 'being moral' with *epoche* applied: bracketing away, suspending, all that we know of human goodness or evil as it manifests itself under the only condition in which we encounter human beings – under social conditions. I argued earlier why it is not prudent to deduce the contents of moral responsibility from the capricious and divergent shapes which various societies stamp over it (Montaigne already said as much, and in a way which left little room for doubt). But nowhere in Levinas will you find the fiction of 'presocial man' or, for that matter, a rather silly idea of a 'presocial state of humanity'.

And so – would we be worse without modernity? I do not know. What I do know is that we would be *different*. Each kind of society legitimizes some varieties of evil, and in all probability 'without modernity' we would be blind to the atrocities which now prompt our disgust and resentment. We still need to wait until a full inventory is made of the atrocities to which modernity made us blind in its turn.

The Levinasian ethic stresses the relationship between the I and the Thou. It is the responsibility of the I to treat the Other as a Thou; as a subject and not as an object. Doesn't this thesis undermine the entire project of social thought? Buber saw that between the I and the Thou is the whole world of the It in which the Other is not approached as a subject of her or his own freedom but, instead, as the member of some category which can only be treated in a way which is, we believe, necessary and inevitable. The It, and everything and anything which makes the Other into an It, thus becomes an obstacle in the way of the recognition of ethical responsibility. The It becomes, in a very real sense, the opposite to the possibility of the ethical.

Now, doesn't this mean that social analysis is thereby inclined by the logic of the presuppositions of this position to identify all social institutions and arrangements as producers or products of the It? Aren't we back to a dichotomy in which society necessarily becomes the world of the unethical It, and the 'before' thus becomes the only chance for responsibility? Doesn't this mean that society and the ethical must, in the end, be identified as distinct?

Most certainly, you have touched here a raw and sore spot in the whole project of a Levinas-inspired correction to the purpose and strategy of social thought. I would not worry that much that it might 'undermine the entire project of social thought', though. I am sure that we will survive this challenge, and I hope that we will emerge from it rejuvenated and reinvigorated as well as wiser, and above all (which counts most) more alert to the pains and miseries of our fellow humans. The worry I share with you entirely follows, in my view, from the strength of Levinas's vision rather than from its weaknesses. The more convincing I find Levinas's vision of morality, the more aware I am of the power of the obstacles piled up on the road to a 'moral society', to a world hospitable to moral leanings and impulses and above all disapproving of itself for being not hospitable enough. To a paper published in *Philosophy Today* in which I vent these worries, I gave the title 'The World Inhospitable to Levinas' (1999c).

As you know, Levinas offers no consistent, let alone convincing, answer to the question of how a moral world can be built starting from the 'moral party of two' and how the 'being for' characteristic of that party can survive (or adjust itself to) the appearance of the Third, that is the entrance of Society. Sociological awareness is not prominent among Levinas's many virtues. He is a nominalist by heart and the 'totality' is never in his thinking 'greater than the sum of its parts'. I suspect that he visualizes 'moral society' as no more, but no less either, than a gathering of moral selves. So he does not supply much leverage to the conviction that society and the ethical are not distinct and that ethics is called and entitled to situate itself above society, as its surveillor and severe judge.

I suspect that the problem of extending moral insights and impulses to society at large (and, most importantly, to the complex network of its institutions) is a matter of *politics*, not morality (hence I perceive my latter-day shift to the examination of politics as the follow-up on Levinasian ethics, not a departure from it), though were we not 'moral beings' answering Levinas's description, we would hardly posit this as a problem and most certainly would not bother with its resolution.

Let me use once again my favourite metaphor, to which I resort whenever I need to make intelligible this confusing mixture of morality's indispensability for the articulation of the task and its ineptitude to fulfil it. Unlike daffodils, we have legs and so can move. Being blessed in addition with language, we can coin an idea of mobility, an idea which would never occur to even the most brainy of legless daffodils. An idea of mobility would not be enough, given the limited capacity of our legs, to carry us to, say, Rome or New York (even, except for the few fittest and exceptionally valiant among us, from Leeds to Portsmouth). What the idea may do (and has done!) is to inspire us to seek, discover or invent 'leg extensions' like railways, boats or planes. Is it not like that with morality, as much our human predicament as walking on legs? We may find the ethical equivalents of rails, ships and jets, and given the fact of being burdened with moral consciences it is unlikely that we will ever stop seeking. The snag is how to translate the moral intuition germinating in the hard-core of the *oikos*, inside the 'moral party of two', into the language of *ecclesia*, and how to 'embody' the translation once it has been made. It is this consideration which prompted me to focus on the *agora*, the home ground of translation. A vigorous *agora*, conscious of its task and earnest about it, seems to be the key to the whole issue. Such an *agora*, alas, is what our society most conspicuously, and most disastrously, lacks.

We have been talking about the ethical dimension in your work up to about 1998. In your books on Globalization, *on* Work, Consumerism and the New Poor *and on* Liquid Modernity, *the ethical dimension has been present as talk about justice. Could you expand a little on what you mean by justice and how that idea (is it a utopia?) can be the basis of an ethical critique of the present.*

I believe that 'justice' is the translation of 'responsibility for', or *Fürsein*, into the language of society. Justice enters ethical concerns the moment the Third appears and with the necessity to compare the degrees of misery and set priorities which that appearance signals but which is never occasioned inside the 'moral party of two'. I believe that 'moral society' is, first and foremost, a *just* society.

But what would the 'just society' be like? The only answer I can offer in good conscience is that a 'just society' is a society which thinks it is not just *enough*, which questions the sufficiency of any achieved level of justice and considers justice always to be a step or more ahead. Above all, it is a society which reacts angrily to any case of *injustice* and promptly sets about correcting it.

I owe to Barrington Moore Jr the idea that by itself 'justice' has no specific meaning, that it 'makes sense' only as a protest against *in*justice. It is injustice which is specific, tangible, obvious though not uncontentious, to be sure. In a society more 'solid' than ours, a society in which forms of life last long enough to spawn standards and sediment habits and routines, what is perceived as 'unjust' is departure from the habitualized ways. Moore has shown that feudal serfs did not mind too much the atrocity of their day-to-day exploitation, but they took to arms the moment the screw was tightened a notch or two: a few hours of extra corvée mattered more and triggered more wrath and resistance than five days a week of obligatory villein service on the lord's fields. Modern capitalism blurred many distinctions, including the distinction between legitimate and illegitimate misery and sent them to the stock exchange of power 'to find their own level'. No longer was the situation as clear-cut as in the times researched by Moore. And yet, in the era of 'hardware' capitalism and 'solid' modernity, standards by which injustice could be measured were incomparably better entrenched and had a much longer life expectation than in our epoch of 'software' capitalism and 'liquid' modernity. For many years, for instance, much of the struggle to rectify injustice was conducted in the defence of wage differentials.

In our times, the concept of injustice is more hotly contested than at any other time in history. It prompts daily reconnaissance skirmishes and recognition wars on ever new fronts. No iniquity is likely to be accepted as 'part of life' for long and borne meekly and placidly. By proxy, also, the idea of justice has become hazier than ever before, and given the mind-boggling pace at which seemingly uncontroversial patterns are rebranded as manifestations of injustice and iniquity, few people would risk committing themselves to blueprints of the 'just society' in the sense of a society thoroughly cleansed of old injustices and giving birth to no new ones.

This is one aspect of the emerging 'liquid modernity' which gives morality grounds for hope. Ever more forms of human misery are reclassified from 'necessary' into 'supernumerary' and excessive, and we all grow ever more impatient with everything so classified. Does this mean that we move closer to the state of 'ultimate justice'? Leaving aside the thorny problem of the endemic inability of any historical form of society to imagine possibilities of a more humane life as reach beyond the horizon set by the worries *presently* experienced, doubts remain as to whether negotiations of better life may ever *in principle* reach their ultimate point and be declared complete. Today's justices tend to be tomorrow's injustices and this 'until-further-notice-ness' is bound to mark them all. A just society as I understand it (that is, a society perpetually vigilant for injustice and never sure that its arrangements are just enough) should seek the best warrant of its staying just in ongoing polyvocality and controversy, not factual or putative consensus.

'Justice', to conclude, can be described only in processual, not static terms. Justice is a horizon which a just society tries to reach, a horizon which moves further away with every step forward that society makes. Insisting on taking such steps and not relenting in this insistence, come what may, are what make a society just.

Is a justice which is demanded in conditions of globalization and in the face of the new poor the same justice which was upheld in classical socialism? Do different conditions imply different justice, or is humiliation an invariant state which always makes the same demands, regardless of time and place?

Yes and no. Humiliation is an 'invariant state'. It is invariantly odious, loathsome and deplorable, though various kinds of people may be humiliated for various kinds of reasons, and though at various times our sensitivity focuses on various kinds of humiliation while always being selective. I would say that as a rule, in any society and at any time, there is more humiliation than this society notices, more still than it admits, and much more than it resolves to alleviate or rectify. This is the prime reason why justice is always outstanding, ahead of everything we do for human well-being and dignity. Conditions that have been branded as contrary to human dignity used for centuries to be suffered in silence by many and passed by with equanimity or without being noticed by others.

The issue of 'moral progress' is admittedly a tricky one, but it seems to me that if we want to measure it at all we should not look to the 'volume of humiliation' – the size of the suffering categories and the execrability of the humiliation they suffer. These things are notoriously difficult to evaluate 'objectively', since the estimates record not so much the amount and depth of pain suffered, as the sufferers' refusal to accept their pain as inevitable, and the agreement of the rest to accept that refusal as legitimate. Paradoxically, it is the public outcry, the more widespread and vociferous the better, an alarm that could easily be mistaken for a symptom of rising injustice, that signals a significant step forward towards justice.

Public sensitivity to, and protest against, humiliation, however, as a rule is selective. At any time, it is certain kinds of humiliation, of certain categories of people, which cause outcry and prompt calls to act, while other kinds are either not admitted as a problem clamouring for resolution, or cast as conditions beyond the human ability to repair, or they are said to be sufferings which cannot be cured or prevented 'from outside' since they are self-inflicted.

We hear a lot about the dominant trend of thought about social realities shifting from 'class' to 'culture'. It seems to me that the shift which has indeed taken place has been wrongly conceptualized in such a formula. What is in fact noticeable these days is the trend to recast class divisions, humiliations and indignities caused by the market-and-property game endemic to the capitalist culture, as 'facts of nature' about which humans, collectively, can do nothing but humbly accept and obey them (through 'laws of the market' which have come to replace the 'laws of history'); while the moral alertness of the public is redirected to focus on the 'claims of recognition' of groups and categories sufficiently resourceful to choose their mode of life and demand its acceptance. Poverty in particular, that class phenomenon *tout court*, is redefined as the self-inflicted pain which socially undertaken relief attempts may only exacerbate (as all foolish attempts to tinker with the laws of nature inevitably do). The poor were present in all known societies, but today's poor are perhaps in more trouble than the poor of yesteryear since, for the first time in history, they have no social function to perform and are for that reason cast outside the scheme of affairs falling into the remit of social action, and beyond the limits of social tasks and societal ambitions. In other words, the perpetuation of poverty no longer offends the sentiments of justice; the battle for justice shifts to other front-lines, never reaching beyond the territory disputed by better armed, more resourceful and resolute camps of free-choosers. The fight for justice may well become a 'family affair' of the successful and well-provided-for; once more, the poor are to be expropriated – this time of their share in the spoils of a justice war. You've picked globalization as a development which may require a certain rethinking of the issue of justice. You are right. The global effects of local actions posit moral responsibilities on a scale which has never before been confronted, let alone coped with. A few decades ago, Hans Jonas pointed to the growing discrepancy between the rapidly expanding temporal and spatial scale of the consequences of high-tech actions and the compass of moral imagination and sensitivity (one may surmise that it is this discrepancy which sociologists try but fail to articulate when they dilute the havoc perpetrated by unbridled and free-floating global forces in the generalistic category of 'unanticipated consequences of human action'). The principle of justice demands responsibility for the consequences one's actions may have on the condition of others, and global power demands global responsibility. The latter, though, is slow to arrive, and when it is awakened it finds itself impotent in the absence of effective agencies capable of acting on its behalf.

The fraction of our incomes we are prepared (and the governments we elect are willing) to share with the far-away peoples impoverished, and deprived of livelihood, as a result of our global search for wealth is pitifully tiny even by comparison with the admittedly inadequate fraction of the national product earmarked for redistribution among the victims of 'economic growth' inside our own societies. The sum of money dedicated thus far to the reconstruction of a Kosovo devastated by Nato bombardments is equal to the costs of one day of the bombing campaign. These are the measures, if you need any, of the 'time lag' of moral imagination in the era of globalization and the degree of 'globality' of moral responsibilities which our societies are prepared to assume. I believe that 'catching up' with the rapidly globalizing economic powers by the political institutions of democratic control, which remain locally confined, constitutes presently the major challenge to the standards of justice and morality; a successive step in the never-ending war for the humanity of human condition.

What do you take to be the practical, everyday implications of the kinds of ethical commitments which are so important in your work?

Few of us are saints, and to demand that all of us be so, and daily, does not seem to be either realistic or, for that matter, morally laudable. Most of us are morally awake most of the time – in small matters. We would help the infirm to cross a busy road, we would rush to help the injured, we would reach for our wallet when shown shocking pictures of victims of a famine or an earthquake. Fortunately, an *experimentum crucis* is not a daily occurrence, and seldom is our moral conscience put to a severe test in which genuine self-sacrifice is required for the sake of others who have no other claims on our generosity except their misery, and who have nothing to offer in exchange. The dense network of conventional stratagems and expedients called 'society' sees to it that this remains a rule of our quotidianity. The problem is, though, 'to keep the powder dry', to accumulate, and preserve, sufficient supplies of moral sensitivity which we may need to draw on in the hour of critical test. Moral sensitivity needs to be excessive to be sufficient: 'in surplus' of what we see as daily, 'ordinary' needs, so that ever new forms of human misery can be perceived as shameful and intolerable cases of indignity and humiliation, and treated accordingly. There is never enough of moral sensitivity, and its cultivation is the preliminary condition of the 'just society', at least in the definition suggested before.

This is the prime reason to be worried. If the 'moral party of two' is the greenhouse of moral sentiments, if it is in that party that the art of 'taking responsibility for one's responsibility' is learned, experimented with, tested and exercised, then the society's capacity for justice depends to a great extent on the quality of 'love relationships' which its culture cultivates. In his beautiful little book on *The Art of Loving,*

Erich Fromm pointed out that in a culture in which the qualities of 'true humility, courage, faith and discipline' are rare, 'the attainment of the capacity to love must remain a rare achievement'. And then he suggested that such rarity is indeed the bane of the society we live in. If 'modern capitalism needs men . . . who consume more and more', if 'man's happiness today consists of "having fun"', if 'the world is one great object for our appetite, a big apple, a big bottle, a big breast' and we are 'the sucklers, the eternally expectant ones, the hopeful ones – and the eternally disappointed ones', then, 'while everybody tries to be as close as possible to the rest, everybody remains utterly alone, pervaded by the deep sense of insecurity, anxiety and guilt which always results when human separatedness cannot be overcome.' In short, the chances of learning the art of love, and thereby coming to appreciate love as a consummate meaning of life and expecting satisfaction from love as a gift rather than gain, are slim.

I regret that we are not all, including myself, saints. Morality may stop short of saintliness. But I am deeply worried that loving may well be on the way to becoming a forgotten, and seldom practised, art. Without that art, there is little hope for morality; and even less for a just society.

Conversation 3

The Ambivalence of Modernity

KEITH TESTER *Why do you think that the debate about modernity and postmodernity emerged in the mid to late 1980s? Was it a product of some crisis in social thought produced by the hegemony of the free market, or was it a sign that all was not well with the old sociological faith in socialism and social transformation? Do you think that the debate emerged because of significant changes in the nature of beauty and humiliation in the world, or did it instead appear as a bright shining illustration of the Columbus complex phenomenon – social thinkers suddenly got bored with their old debates and started to look enviously at what they took to be the greener grass over the fence in the gardens of the artists and so forth?*

ZYGMUNT BAUMAN I do not think there are rules by which the *coining* of new concepts abides, but I suspect that the *acceptance* of new concepts, and particularly the widespread acceptance, and most of all a widely and wildly enthusiastic acceptance, is indeed rule-abiding. New concepts are avidly sought and joyfully welcomed when a feeling grows that the realities which the previously used concepts stood for and pointed to have changed and will go on changing profoundly enough to need a new rubric: that the old concept tends to the aspects of realities which are no longer central and offers an axis around which the current experience no longer rotates. You could take a hint from Thomas Kuhn and speak of the longing for 'paradigm change', if sociology were like natural science, where objects of scientific processing are timeless by comparison with the ways of studying them, and it is mostly the dynamic activity of the scholars that turns out 'anomalies' in ever greater quantity, sooner or later reaching a 'critical volume'. However, in our sociological profession the objects tend to be much more dynamic than our efforts to grasp them and than the conceptual nets which we weave for that purpose. My guess is that in the eighties I was not alone in desperately looking for a new cognitive frame into which our fast-changing image of the shared human world would fit better than it did in the one proffered by the 'orthodox consensus'. The profligacy of the 'post' words, the conspicuous mark of those years, testified to a 'betwixt and between' state of sociological reason: most of us felt that something quite crucial for the extant imagery had been left behind or fallen by the board, but we were far from ready to pinpoint with any degree of confidence whatever came to replace it. This may be a characteristic trait of the modern mind: that it can grasp the nature of the present solely in its difference from what is assumed to be its past, though the typically modern form of 'false consciousness' is to seek the definition of the present in its supposed future-aimed trends.

'Postmodernity' was one possibility among such concepts. It was badly needed, intuitively longed for and desperately sought. To me, it seemed more felicitous than other 'posts' on offer. Since it engaged both the changing world and its reflection in human experience, it allowed a focus on the ongoing transformations affecting the way in which sociological reason was for the duration of modern times situated in social realities, and so on the nature of strategies which could be usefully pursued in sociological thought. *Legislators and Interpreters* was an attempt to capture that intertwining of social transformation and its intellectual reflection, linked by the shifting location of those who did the reflecting or strove to articulate and systematize its intuitions.

The category of people later (quite late in their collective history, as a matter of fact) to be called 'intellectuals', people professionally engaged in the business of reflection aimed at 'making sense' (whatever may be the currently deployed distinction between 'sense' and 'nonsense'), were from the beginning of the modern era cast in the role of legislators. That role was perfectly tuned to the *Zeitgeist* of modern living. 'Being modern' means to be in a state of perpetual modernization: modernity is, so to speak, the time of 'new beginnings' and of forever new 'new beginnings', of dismantling old structures and building new ones from scratch. There is a tendency to speak in retrospect of the 'project of modernity': I am not sure that there was such a project, *the* project *of modernity*, but I believe that what set the modern era apart from other times was the obsession with designing and pursuing projects, the tendency to subordinate the present – each successive present – to the project yet to be fulfilled. Habermas's 'unfinished project' is, in fact, a definition of modernity as such. It all started, after all, from the victory of the 'moderns' in their *querelle* with the 'ancients' who insisted that mankind reached the peak of its glory long ago, and that the best it can do now is emulate past achievements as well as it can manage.

Projects could be and were many, and they kept changing well before coming anywhere near being finished. But there was hardly ever a moment with no project, or rather with no competing projects. Each project could be contested, but never the *need of projects*. Modernity took off once the *ancien régime* – that self-reproducing order, that order reproducing itself unreflexively and therefore unaware of being a problem and a task, in fact, of being an 'order' – fell apart, and one premise underlying all modernity's works was the 'without us, a deluge' axiom: things cannot be left to themselves, lest a disaster (chaos, *bellum omnium contra omnes*, law of the jungle) should prevail. The drawing board was one contraption modernity could not exist without, and the profession of designer, of drafter of blueprints, was the best entrenched of modern vocations, one that emerged intact from all and any changes of style and fashion. Modern society had an insatiable thirst for legislating, defining norms, setting standards; for beauty, goodness, truth, propriety, usefulness and happiness. It probably helped to keep that activity going forever that all such standards were set in the future, that non-existing condition (the 'absolute alterity', as Levinas pointed out) which cannot be empirically examined and therefore can never supply grounds for proving or disproving any assertion.

Under the circumstances, the 'legislating' job of the 'reflecting classes' was self-evident. The sociologists (or rather the sociologically minded) among them strove to legislate for the job of legislating: for the power structures capable of legislating and of legislating effectively, that is of ensuring that the laws once stated will be obeyed. 'Society' for social thinkers was a shorthand for 'nation-state', that simultaneously cultural (nation) and political (state) agency. With the help of this agency and its legislating powers, the really-existing society could be gradually, yet resolutely, brought up to the exacting standards of 'good society': a just society, the reason-guided society, a setting for secure and happy humanity; indeed a 'perfect' society, in the sense that no further change would be possible or required to improve it.

I suppose that it was the collapse of this agency which suggested, contrary to the established belief, that modernity after all could be itself a historical phenomenon rather than the final stage of history; that modernity may have an 'end', that there is a 'post' *after* the modern adventure. Such an idea would have hardly occurred to the 'reflecting classes' were it not for the sight of the state shedding, one after another, its ambitions of introducing the 'perfect society by design'; of the state ceding its functions to the admittedly chaotic, un- or underregulated 'blind' forces of competition; of the avidly deregulating state actively promoting instead of fighting 'flexibility', as the forces once feared and resented as randomness, contingency and chaos have been renamed. The unintended, yet inevitable, outcome of deregulation and the abandonment of managerial ambitions was a rehabilitation of disorder, that public enemy number one which for a couple of centuries spurred the ruling as well as the reflecting classes into action.

Schumpeter wouldn't prognosticate the survival of modern capitalist order. Capitalism, he believed, would be stifled sooner or later by the stiff hierarchy of bureaucratic command. That the future would entail planning and ever more planning, management and ever more management, that the society of the future, whatever else it could be, would be an *administered* society, was the belief 'beyond left and right' and hardly ever questioned, even by those members of the 'reflecting classes' who, like Adorno or Arendt, did not enjoy the prospect of it and resented what they saw as the 'totalitarian tendency', or who, like Lukàcs, proclaimed that 'totality is false.' It was such expectations that were belied in the 'deregulation' era. The state ceding its tasks to the market gave the lead, but the tendency to shed managerial responsibilities penetrates all sectors of social life, the whole of the life-setting. It seems that bureaucracy, which Weber had every reason to project as the embodiment of modernity and its endemic rationality, has had its day, much like totalitarian ambitions, 'iron grips', inflexible hierarchies of command and panoptical techniques of domination.

From its inception, modernity was known in one form only: that of 'managerial' modernity, an order-designing and order-administering modernity. No wonder that in the light of new experience the idea of modernity grinding to a halt seemed credible and the advent of *post* modernity, the time when the works of modernity would come to be taken apart and the 'project of modernity' abandoned, was announced.

That 'after' bit which the concept of 'postmodernity' entailed seemed to me suspicious from the start. Could one take the retreat from the 'total-order-designing' ambitions, and the collapse of the agency capable of carrying out such ambitions, for the 'end of modernity'? Is not modernity about incessant and obsessive *modernization*, about Carroll's need to 'run much faster to stay put', rather than about any particular destination of the running and the method of staying on the track? Is the fate of modernity tied to one historical form or is not the rejection of that form and embarking once more on a 'new beginning' rather a sign of modernity's health and vigour? The news of modernity's demise was, in other words, grossly exaggerated. It seemed to me that the 'postmodern perspective' which allowed the scrutiny of modernity's failures and the debunking of many of its undertakings as blind alleys, far from being in opposition to modernity or growing on its grave, had from the start been its indispensable *alter ego*: that restless, perpetually dissentful voice that enabled modernity to succeed in its critical engagement with found reality and the many realities sedimented by that engagement. I liked Lyotard's quip: one cannot be truly modern without first being postmodern.

The 'time of postmodernity' is to me the time in which the postmodern stance has come to know itself, and 'knowing itself' means the realization that the critical job has no limits and could never reach its terminal point; that, in other words, the 'project of modernity' is not just 'unfinished', but *unfinishable*, and that this 'unfinishability' is the essence of the modern era. As you know, I tried to express that idea when defining postmodernity as 'modernity minus its illusions'. Not that illusions have been finished once for all. I wonder to what extent the indefatigable proliferation of modern projects depends on the stubbornness, recurrent resurrections and successive reincarnations of the illusions of the 'last stand', of the 'this time for sure'. Every time a new and untried technology for tackling and bending and streamlining the recalcitrant and messy reality beckons, one hears the prophecies of 'ultimate solutions'. Sloterdijk's is the most recent example.

But what exactly is modernity? Is modernity the theory and the practice of humans making society for ourselves, without looking over our shoulders for supernatural advice? Is it the principle that we are 'self-sufficient'?

Yes, indeed. I agree. But I would add that there was a mixture of 'we can' and 'we must' in that belief in self-sufficiency. We cannot but be self-sufficient *because* we have been abandoned to our own cunning and our own, however scarce, resources. Michael Allen Gillespie has recently published a splendid study showing the direct link between the Franciscan/Nominalist God as an essentially wilful, omnipotent and for that reason unknowable Supreme Being, and the 'self-confidence by necessity' which led to the spectacular outburst of modern creativity. The God of the Fraticelli or Ockham was in Gillespie's description capricious, 'fearsome in his power, unknowable, unpredictable, unconstrained by nature and reason, and indifferent to good and evil'. With *Deus* for all practical intents and purposes *absconditus* – retired from the daily worries of the humans, and invisible – there would be little point in wishing to fathom His verdicts. There is nothing left but to try to compose one's life as decently and as well as one can manage. 'Science does not need to take God or Scripture into account in its efforts to come to terms with the natural world' – but, let me add, the alternative would be a sheer waste of time. Freedom from the direct interference of God recalled more a sinister fate than man's victory. God created humans to eke out their own existence: to self-create. They may have insufficient powers and wits to fulfil that task to their satisfaction, but there is nothing else to be done but try. The Renaissance could celebrate the freshly discovered powers of self-creation, but there was a solid measure of 'there is no alternative' resignation in that joy. 'Like the God who created him, this man is an artisan, but an artisan whose greatest work of art is himself.' There would not be any 'himself' were the artisanship unpractised. In the human predicament, freedom to choose is a no-choice matter.

In other words, what was determined by The Creator was human indeterminacy. Not self-sufficiency: that had still to be achieved, and achieving it, plausible or not, feasible or not, is bound to remain the 'essence' of human-being-in-the-world. You may say that modernity is a long and continuous bid for such self-sufficiency. Alain Peyrefitte suggested that behind the astonishing dynamics of the frames and forms of modern life stood *confidence*: confidence in one's own powers, in the conduct of others (Giddens would use here the concept of 'trust': expectation that most of the time and under most circumstances the others would refrain from breaching the rules one would expect them to follow), and confidence in the institutions – their solidity, longevity, reliability and ability to deliver.

All three pillars of confidence today seem to be shaky and wobbly. My guess is that the new infirmity of the first two is an after-effect of the dilapidation of the third, of institutional trust. I think that rather than speak of three pillars or three dimensions we should better visualize the relations between the three kinds of confidence as those between a trunk and two branches: confidence in oneself and in others growing out of the confidence in the toughness and perpetuity of institutions. Only solid institutions with a life expectation much longer than that of individual life projects may serve as reference points and frames for individual planning and offer that modicum of certainty ('grip on the present', as Bourdieu would put it) without which any planning, let alone long-term planning, is inconceivable. Most of modern history was dedicated to the construction and servicing of such a tough, steady, long-living institutional framework for confident individual action (this is what the modern concerns with 'order' were, ultimately, about). It is that framework which is now falling apart; few if any institutions are left which can be confidently expected to last longer than it takes to fulfil bolder, farther-reaching plans, let alone a 'whole-life project' of the kind still recommended a few decades ago by Jean-Paul Sartre, and new institutions tend to be born with the stigma of transience and with an 'until further notice' clause in their birth certificates. One feels tempted to say that 'society' is now on the way out from the world of daily life, following the example of the Franciscan/Nominalist God. Like that God, 'society', which used to loom large in the human *Weltanschauung* as the supreme lawgiver and the ultimate judge of the propriety of individual pursuits, appears 'capricious, fearsome in its power, unknowable, unpredictable, unconstrained by nature and reason, and indifferent to good and evil'; just one crafty and guileful player among many, rather than a strict and impartial Judge. The collapse of confidence in the conduct of others is the effect, soon to be followed by doubts of the increasingly disoriented selves as to their own power to design and control the course of their lives.

Your account of modernity stresses the problem of order and of ordering designs. Why is this? Why don't you emphasize industrialism or capitalism? Why order?

I believe that the preoccupation with order, or with an orderly, manageable society, is a common denominator of other modern undertakings: industrialism, capitalism, democracy. Through somewhat different means the same ends have been pursued. The longing for human-made order lubricated the wheels of the three 'society-targeted' modern pursuits. Their coordination was far from perfect, the conflicts have long been noted and amply recorded, but the three roads converged on a regular, predictable and controllable human habitat as its imagined/desired destination. What I am saying is not just 'with the benefit of hindsight': if we had more time to discuss this, I would show that the desire to manipulate probabilities and to make human affairs regular and amenable to planning and control was high up in the mind of the principal advocates and actors of industrialism, democracy and, incredibly, capitalism (remember Hirschman's findings: the passion of gain seen as the weapon to tame, neutralize and render harmless all the rest of the passions blamed for the messiness of life in common).

I think that modernity and the *awareness* of the artificiality of social order are synonymical. The characteristically modern obsession with ordering is the outcome of that awareness. It makes a lot of difference to take order as a verdict of God, nature or history (more correctly, to fail to perceive 'order' as a separate issue), or to see it as a task which needs to be urgently undertaken and doggedly pursued.

A point which comes across very strongly in your book Modernity and Ambivalence *is that of the side-effects of the modern ordering ambitions and designs. You show that the designs for a perfect order do not lead to a moment of rest when the designers can sit back and admire the perfect world that they have created. In human terms, the imposition of order leads to the identification of groups of people who do not fit the designs, and, as the designs have to be improved in order to deal with the putative disorder and disorderly, so ever wider groups who do not fit the exact pattern are found. This means that certain groups become identified by the order-makers as problems. They also become outsiders from the point of view of the designers of order; they become strangers who should not be 'in here' because they are not 'like us'. In European modernity the archetypical group 'not like us' was identified as the Jews. In other words, you are saying that designs of order and purity create ambivalence. These are very big questions, but could you clarify your concept of ambivalence and explain precisely why, in European modernity, the Jews tended to be identified in terms of this problematic presence?*

I believe that as modern times proceed, more and more of our ordering efforts are targeted at the unwanted outcomes of past ordering efforts. Ivan Illich gave an excellent example of that rule by tracing the dynamics of modern medicine, ever more concerned with antidotes against ailments caused by medical interventions into other afflictions.

The purpose of ordering is the elimination of situational ambiguity and behavioural ambivalence. The point, though, is that the fit between the conceptual grid (ordering always entails dividing and classifying) serving as the design for the future orderly reality, and the 'really existing reality' to be remade in the likeness of that grid, is seldom if ever perfect. For that reason, almost every ordering measure brings into being new ambiguities and ambivalences which call for further measures, and the chase never ends. Mary Douglas argued this case beautifully in *Purity and Danger* (though she stopped short of postulating the endemic inconclusiveness of the war against ambivalence). But you can find a similar argument in Edmund Leach: pun, obscenity, blasphemy, just like other, non-linguistic varieties of 'taboo', are symptoms of the incurable 'non-fit' between vocabulary with its delimited semantic fields and a not-so-discrete and neatly sliced reality. 'Taboo', described by ethnographers as manifestations of superstitious, irrational minds when found among distant (and 'inferior', 'culturally backward') peoples, are in fact the inevitable supplement of the effort of rationalization.

Ambiguous beings, sending ambivalent signals, are such as span categories meant to be kept separate and needing separation to preserve the clarity of behavioural rules. Ambiguous beings are 'monsters', unlike any other beings whose handling causes no confusion and no hesitation. They cannot be treated the way the other, 'normal' beings are (that is, those neatly fitting one, and only one, of the classes into which the world phenomena are split). In *Modernity and the Holocaust* I suggested that inside Christendom, Jews were such monsters: they trespassed over the sacrosanct boundary between the Catholic and the heathens, thereby implying its arbitrariness. Jews managed to be both at the same time: Christianity's elder brothers who became pagan by choice, rejecting Christ's divine mission. They were unlike any 'normal' people, legitimate dwellers of the world created as the object of the converting and redeeming mission of the church. Like all other monsters, they evoked reactions as ambivalent as they themselves were ambiguous. They were the most abject and detestable of creatures, but at the same time carriers of awesome though obscure powers. I think that the attitude endemic to Christianity was one of *allo*semitism (Latin *allus* – other), rather than *anti*semitism: no ordinary norms can be applied to the Jews, Jews are unlike any other humans and call to be set apart from all others by being subjected to a treatment devised for them alone.

Christendom bequeathed the Jews to the modern world as ambivalence incarnate: they were, so to speak, made to the measure of all future demands for the embodied targets of crusades against ambivalence in its new forms, conjured up by modern ordering zeal. In the Europe of princes, Jewish cross-boundary kinship networks made 'King's Jews' into an asset whenever go-betweens were needed to resolve dynastic disputes; in the Europe of nations that followed, the same 'out-of-placenessness' of the Jews made them into a liability, but also a direct threat against the territorial aspirations of the budding and not-so-well-assured national homelands. In the Europe that called humans to define themselves by their nationality, Jews and Gypsies were the sole 'non-national nations', a blot scattered all over the emerging order. These were not, though, the only doors closing on the road to order in which Jews shoved their fingers. The Jews had been prefabricated as a ready-made container capacious enough to accommodate any ambivalence currently in the front-line (I have documented this case in the book in more detail and see no need to repeat the argument here). In the world of races, as visualized by Hitler, Jews were not a 'race apart'. They were, as always, monsters, the only race which refused to 'stick to its own kind' but instead spilled over all the places belonging to others. If monsters erode the identity of species, the monstrous 'anti-race' of the Jews sapped the identities of races right and proper.

Does it follow that ambivalence, more or less by definition, implies the humiliation of being treated as 'not like us', as a 'problem to be overcome in the name of order' running alongside a certain freedom and emancipation from the conceit that 'there is no alternative' and therefore of an attenuated appreciation of the possibilities of the creation of beauty? I am not, however, wanting to say something as crass as that the creation of beauty in some way redeems the suffering and humiliation; it does not.

The fighters against ambiguous others are drawn into battle by the vexing experience of the ambivalence which they would dearly wish to stamp down or quash; those at the receiving end of their fight are, mirror-like, exposed to contradictory pressures and drawn in mutually opposed directions. Again, I've analysed the latter predicament in some detail in *Modernity and Ambivalence* and would not wish to risk here an uncalled-for simplification of a complex picture. In the book I focused on assimilatory pressures, a norm in the era of nation-building and the entrenchment of the modern state: the two processes were rolled into one as nationalism, eagerly deployed by the nascent states as a prime means to extract the desired volume of loyalty and obedience. The countless ethnic, linguistic, cultural and regional groupings enclosed within state borders were cajoled or forced voluntarily to renounce their separate identities and merge into the unified, homogenous body of the nation: were they to try to oblige however, and try with zeal and ardour, they would be suspected of dishonesty and ignoble intentions. Nationalist mythology posits nationhood as a matter of shared history, and 'common stock' as a quality which cannot be freely chosen and is not the genuine article unless bearing the mark of 'primordiality'. The line dividing nationalism, demanding cultural unity, from racism, proclaiming natural grounds for that unity, could not but be tenuous, and the sight of people 'unlike us' flocking to join the nation reshaped into a state must have been worrying and off-putting for the defenders of the national myth. People whose ancestors were not present at the mythical and invariably ancient birth of the nation had no right to the insiders' status; were that status to be granted, the grounds for demanding unquestionable loyalty to the nation's heritage and destiny would be sapped. What can be freely chosen can also be freely abandoned. Nationalism was haunted by an endemic contradiction that could not but rebound in highly ambivalent policies towards the 'others inside', waiting to be projected on to the targets of those policies.

It was these targets, the 'others inside', the 'in, but not of', who had to drink from the river of ambivalence. They were drawn by an offer they could not (and many would not) resist, and they were repelled by the suspicions and mistrust of the issuers of the invitation. Whether they rejected or embraced the offer, whatever they said and did would promptly be taken down and could be used against them once their conduct came to be judged. The rules of the game cast them in a no-win position, and there seemed to be no escape from humiliation; a continuous humiliation, and a lot of it, daily apportioned.

Being in that position meant incapacitation, legal disempowerment and cultural disablement. Their own forms of life tended to be devalued and denigrated, while the forms of life brandished as superior stayed tantalizingly out of reach. The resulting void was an utterly unpleasant place to inhabit, but it also gave its residents a chance to see through what the others, the occupants of more benign and safer places, could not or would not penetrate: to spot contingency beyond the no-appeal-allowed verdicts of fate, human choices beyond historical necessities – indeed, the liquidity of human condition beneath the thin crust of apparently solid institutions. The chance did not *have* to be taken, but it *could*, and it *was* taken by many. The 'betwixt and between' is the right place from which to examine and contemplate the complex geology of the shores.

The times of assimilatory pressures seem to have passed, at least in our part of the planet, together with the sovereign states seeking ideological mobilization to exact discipline with cultural domination and cultural crusades, with massive conversions, chronopolitics and credible claims to cultural superiority. Ambivalence did not disappear, though, from life experience. For an overwhelming majority of us it has become instead the daily bread. The ambiguity of human condition no longer pretends to be but an unlucky departure from normality and a temporary irritant. As a matter of fact, the recently common tendency to substitute 'emic' (expulsionist) strategies for the 'fagic' (assimilatory) ones which were widespread in the times of nation-state building, the tendency towards forceful separation, repulsion of migrants and ethnic cleansing is an oblique and perverse admission that this is indeed the case; that ambivalence cannot be

resolved or overcome. The currently fashionable 'emic' strategies are, however, bound to share the lot of the 'fagic'
predecessors which are now running out of steam and out of
fashion. Currently, the most powerful stream of existential
ambiguity and behavioural ambivalence springs from the
multiplicity of authorities, the plurality of life forms and
polyvocality – all permanent, irremovable ingredients of
'liquid modernity' times. As before, ambivalence is itself an
incurably ambiguous predicament and a profoundly ambivalent experience: it portends humiliation, yet augurs excep-
tional opportunity for the seekers of beauty, for cultural and
intellectual creation.

*One of the main debates about the Holocaust is whether it was
a peculiarly German invention or whether a Holocaust could
have been perpetrated by any modern state given the imposition
of a dream of pure order and the opportunity to work towards
the realization of that dream without let or hindrance. The
question is whether the fact that the Holocaust was perpetrated
primarily by Germany is a result of some special and unique
path of development followed by Germany but by no other
European state. This is the* Sonderweg *thesis. Meanwhile your
Holocaust book tends to be quite clear that the Holocaust only
happened in Germany because of contingent circumstances. It
could be argued that the logic of your account of the Holocaust
is to downplay its German aspect and instead to emphasize the
culpability of modernity. Is the story of the perpetration of the
Holocaust a chapter in the history of Germany or of modernity?*

People were murdered for the sin of belonging to the wrong
kind of group long before modernity took off. The Pope has
recently apologized for the 'categorial murders' committed
by the Christian church (or in its name). The victims were
infidels, people who rejected the true faith. In most cases,
though, at least as a matter of principle, they were offered
the chance of recantation and atonement. They were sen-
tenced to death for what they *did*, not for what they *were*.
Paradoxically, premodern genocides were oblique recogni-

tions of the victims' free will. Equally paradoxically, in our modern times, in which the praise of free will is daily sung and the message of free choice is hammered home at every turn, genocide justifies itself in terms which deny the victims' freedom of choice. Russian and Ukrainian 'kulaks' might have earnestly abstained from wrong-doing, but what they could not choose was to stop being 'kulaks' or having been born in a 'kulak' family. German Jews could go out of their way wholeheartedly to embrace gentile ways and means, but what they had no power to change was their Jewishness, predetermined by Jewish origin. There is nothing that Albanians in Kosovo could do yesterday to stop being Albanians, nor is there anything the Serbs in Kosovo can do today to stop being Serbs. Tutsi cannot be Hutu, Hutu cannot turn into Tutsi. Their identity has been written down in their passports and their original and unredeemable sin is to have been so recorded.

It is essentially a modern invention that for certain categories of human beings there is, simply, no room in the 'good society' about to be built, not because of their wrong-doings but because of their incapacity of doing right. A modern variety of criminals, the by-product of the ordering ambitions, are categories of people whose crime consists in having been accused. We may laugh at certain accusations, collect proofs showing that some other charges are ungrounded, we may exonerate some of the accused and pity some others. But the priority of garden design over 'really existing gardens', the idea that some types of humans may be of a 'weedy nature' and bound to remain such, that some sorts of *Leben* are *unwertes*, that the beings burdened with certain features better, for the sake of the design, be removed altogether or better still prevented from being born, is deeply ingrained in the modern mind and crops up over and over again in ever new avatars.

I never said (nor thought) that Germany is not guilty of the Holocaust crime. I only said, repeatedly (and will go on repeating) that Germany's guilt is not a German affair, that Germany did what it did because of what it *shares* with the rest of us, not because of what makes it different from us, and that therefore the most bloodcurdling of all the lessons of the Holocaust is not that 'this could happen to us', but that 'we could do it, given the right circumstances.' The *Endlosung* was a laboratory in which the capacities of our civilization, set to reach perfection through eliminating such beings as are short of being perfect, have been put to an *experimentum crucis*. It is just one of the modern capacities, and there is no 'historical inevitability' of it leading to a Holocaust. But without modern civilization, without the whole assortment of its achievements of which we are otherwise so proud, the Holocaust which did happen in Germany would have been unthinkable.

The trouble with blaming Germany and its *Sonderweg* is that everybody else is exonerated. What is forgotten then is that the essential ideas of 'racial stock' and eugenic (race-improving) policies were invented, acquired scientific credentials and received public acclaim far outside German borders; that they had been implemented, with ardour, long before the Nazis came to power (notably in the USA), and long after the burned-up cadaver of Hitler was found in the *Reichkanzlei* courtyard (notably in all Scandinavian countries, under the supervision of social-democratic governments); that Hitler, fond of representing himself as the executor of mankind's ambitions, never had any difficulty in producing long lists of luminaries of modern thought to support his ideas of the 'good society' and his way of implementing them; and that Vichy rulers pushed through anti-Jewish laws which went far beyond German legislation, that they did it on their own initiative and without any German nudging, and whatever they did was done in the name of the 'healthy, resurrected France', not for the sake of the German race's world rule. I believe that all this can be forgotten only at our own peril. Getting rid of *unwertes Leben*, and pronouncing confidently which life is worth living and which is not, are constant temptations of modern times, and it would be naive as well as ethically horrifying to be unaware of the need to hold this temptation in check

and be vigilant enough to perceive its workings in our day-
to-day cravings, particularly those which are apparently
innocuous because they are hiding under ostensibly noble
names and for that reason hallowed by some, swallowed
placidly by others.

In our times this *desideratum* acquires even more urgency
than it carried before. And this is not because the threat of
Endlosung-style moves has increased. The contrary is the
case, since a condensed and streamlined operation like the
Holocaust would require a state power sovereign and centralized to a degree unlikely to be reached again. The
totalitarian tendency so prominent in 'solid' modernity wilts
and dissipates in the 'liquid' variant of the modern condition.
Learning the true lessons of the Holocaust acquires new and
enhanced importance precisely for the opposite reasons: like
so many other aspects of the modern condition, the temptation which I mentioned a moment ago has been left out of
state administration, deregulated and privatized, to follow
the pattern of currencies or wages and 'find its own level'
amidst market competition. In its new rendition it could be
easily misrecognized – or recognized belatedly – when the
devastation will already have been done. The idea that the
right to live is not a birthright (or pre-birth right for that
matter), that it can and should be set against other people's
right to happiness and freedom from worry and sacrificed to
the 'greater good' (or the good of the more resourceful),
appears today in the disguise of the individual's 'freedom of
choice', a value as unanimously applauded today as the
value of 'rational society' was a century ago, and as such has
seldom a chance to be examined and questioned. But it is
the old sinister temptation all the same, and left to be
exploited by commercial markets instead of the 'Total
States' of yesteryear it stands every chance of being vented
more widely and effectively than ever before. Human genes
are already in private firms' ownership, but in the name of
the consumer's freedom to choose, as well as the right to
choose one's company, having decided first (or accepted the
mediatic summaries of the 'common sense') what sort of

company is worth having and what sort of humans are unworthy to be sociated with.

It can be suggested that the fact that you spoke about the Holocaust and modernity itself demonstrated that you were thinking and writing from a position outside of modernity. At the time, you would have identified that position as one of ambivalence between the modern and the postmodern. But what are we to understand by 'postmodernity'?

After *Deus absconditus*, which started off the modern confidence in the powers of the human *species*, came *Societas abscondita*, which triggered the postmodern confidence in the powers of human *individuals*. In both cases, let me repeat, there was a touch of despair in the confidence, the 'there is nothing else we can do' feeling; since appeal to the wardens and guardians up there is likely to have all the effects of crying in the wilderness, let us stop wasting time and concentrate instead on what we can do, collectively or singly, with our own hands, and let us hope that we get more skills and make better tools in order to use our hands more efficiently and with more satisfying results.

Perhaps God has His designs for the future, but spending precious energy to penetrate His plans would bring little gain anyway. Perhaps history has its logic, but guessing what that logic is would not help much anyway. And so, let us take one thing at a time and start worrying how to cross the next bridge when we come to it. We can say that postmodern time is not an arrow. It has lost the pointer which was the mark of modern time. But I think it is better to say that we've stopped guessing where the arrow points. Time flows, and flows faster than ever before, but we can no longer plot the riverbed which keeps it on a predetermined course, even if there is one. If modernity was busy 'disembedding' individuals from their received settings, it did so in order to 're-embed' them more securely than ever before; to create 'structures' built on design and more solid than the cramped and uncomfortable, shabby and unreliable frames left by the *ancien régime.* Postmodernity (modernity in its 'liquid' phase) is the era of disembedding without re-embedding. Any frames that are constructed are meant to serve as vehicles to keep on the move as long as it takes to reach the next halfway inn, not as homes in which to rest at the end of the road.

Postmodern time (or, as I prefer to express it now, the 'liquid modern' time) is cut into episodes which do not come in any consistent logical order. They seem to be amenable to all sorts of reshuffling. Their succession is in no way preordained, it is more like the order of beads on a string. Luc Boltanski and Eve Chiapello suggest that the model we all tend to carry in our heads these days is one of *cité par projets* (the plural of the last term is crucially important in this phrase): the profusion of fixed-term projects and the hope that the range of choice will go on growing rather than diminishing replace the allure and the motivational power of the one and only *projet de la vie*, the 'whole life' project. Each successive 'project' that is undertaken must be seen through and fulfilled to the best of one's ability solely in order to demonstrate the performer's 'capacity of fulfilling projects', and to secure his or her *employability* when it comes to the allocation and appropriation of the next batch of projects. A merry-go-round comes to mind rather than marathon running; a life as a string of rounds, a sequence of new starts, often in unconnected places and unrelated surroundings. Keeping fit for the next, yet unknown round, whatever it may be, is the main achievement, revocable as the rest.

One can think of the difference between 'solid' and 'liquid' contexts of modern life also from the perspective of the changing nature of the experiment, that crucial expedient in the strategy of beings obliged to work out their own destiny. The inherited meaning of an experiment was an attempt to find out how a certain end could best be achieved. Not just the objective, but different ways of achieving it were adumbrated, and the experimenting went on so long as the best way had not been found. We are all perforce experimenters, but the order of ends and means has been reversed. We tend to go on trying different applications of the skills, talents and other resources which we have, suspect we have or hope to have, and try to find out which result brings most satisfaction. Such experimenting, however, has no built-in endpoint; findings are never conclusive, 'most satisfaction *so far*' does not mean 'most satisfaction possible', and so there is no such thing as 'the final proof' of anything, and experimenting must go on.

If in 'solid modernity', bent on producing solid, unbreakable beds for the 'disembedded' to 're-embed', the royal road to success was to conform, to fit into a prefabricated bed, in 'liquid modernity' the secret of success is not to be unduly conservative, to refrain from habitualizing to any particular bed, be mobile and perpetually at hand. To prove that one is the 'genuine article' one needs to be flexible, always at a beck and call, ready to start anew, rather than conform and stick to the form once it has been taken.

There seems to be a striking resonance, or if you wish a 'selective kinship', between direction-less history and project-less biography.

Is there a difference between modern and postmodern order?

Oh yes, there are differences, and aplenty; difficult to decide where to start! Pierre Bourdieu many years ago spotted the shift in the ways in which discipline is elicited and social integration pursued: from normative regulation to seduction, from policing to public relations, from enforcement to advertising. I think that what underpins all such changes is the ceding of the task of social integration by the centralized and closely administered agencies to dispersed and essentially uncoordinated 'market forces'. Myself, I suggested the retreat of the panoptical techniques of domination, discarded not so much for their moral hideousness as for their exorbitant costs and above all for preventing or constraining the mobility of the dominant as much as they confine the freedom of the dominated. These techniques have been by and large (except in the treatment of the criminalized margins, where direct hour-by-hour surveillance is still preferred) abandoned and replaced by what Pierre Bourdieu has recently called 'the policy of precarization': disabling the dominated by the threat of the exodus of the dominating, a decision which would leave them to their own sorely inadequate resources.

The link between domination and territorial conquest and administration, so intimate in the time of 'solid' modernity, has been broken. In the power struggle of our days the appropriation of territory has shifted from asset to liability, again for its adverse effects: the immobilization of the dominant, tying them down to the endless, cumbersome responsibilities which the administration of a territory inevitably entails. In the era of planetary mobility and planet-wide networks of instantaneous communication, 'garrisons in the conquered cities' seem blatantly useless as much as they are prohibitively costly. One tends much more often to hear today of the withdrawal of troops than of invasions (at least in the globalizing, as distinct from the globalized, part of the world).

It all boils down to the passage from engagement to *disengagement*, performed or contemplated as the principal strategy of power struggle, domination, law-and-order servicing and social integration (as well as, by more than a mere coincidence, of life politics), a phenomenon which I have already invoked several times in our conversations. On conditions of life, that passage has an impact which is difficult to exaggerate. Uncertainty and insecurity have not just turned from a temporary irritant into an endemic feature of a 'no alternative' existence, but they have been deployed now as the paramount vehicle of systemic integration, if not of social cohesion. This shift cannot but generate enormous volumes of tension and anxiety, which the nation-states, the traditional agencies designed to deal with this sort of thing, are neither resourceful enough nor, indeed, willing to alleviate, let alone cut at the roots.

There are no evident cures for the state of uncertainty and anxiety, and so the sources of tension and anxiety are unlikely to dry up. Unable to reach things that truly matter, the energy so generated tends to be redirected to the objects close at hand, such things as one seems to be able to do something about: first and foremost, to the concerns with the safety of the body and its immediate surroundings. The strangers nearby are the obvious targets; the close-to-home, visible and tangible outposts of all those elusive, mysterious, difficult to pinpoint and impenetrable, and above all unpredictable, forces which play havoc with all habitual routines, frustrate life plans and thwart the very effort to plan. More often than not, politicians are glad and eager to oblige. The notion of 'asylum seekers' fast becomes a term of abuse, immigration and naturalization laws are tightened, the setting up of 'detention centres' (the sanitized name for discredited concentration camps) becomes a plank of electoral platforms, hoped to attract more votes than any other promise. Given the overall weakening of the 'undivided sovereignty' of the state, 'final solutions' in our part of the world are unlikely to be perpetrated. There is no force able to plan them, administer and see them through. We may expect more forceful ghettoizations and wall-building and Dover-style anti-immigrant riots rather than new Auschwitzes.[1] Tribal sentiments, unlike nation-state policies, are prone to lead to scattered eruptions of violence rather than the systematic extermination of stigmatized culprits of anxiety; to use Juri Lotman's metaphor, the probable manifestations of anxiety will be more akin to the random explosions on a minefield rather than to the awesome flow of a river gathering force on the way to the estuary.

What differences do you identify between modern and postmodern ethics?

The question is no doubt pertinent, alas the answer is not easy. Having written a book called *Postmodern Ethics* I feel perhaps more distant from finding an answer than I otherwise would be. We may say with a modicum of certainty what the modern ethics was about (finding a code of behaviour which every sound-minded person would have to follow), what the ethical practice of modernity was about (legislating a social setting which would leave the person no choice but to obey the code), what the benefits of that practice were (diminishing the volume of violence, that is of illegitimate – unauthorized – coercion, in daily life), at what price those benefits had been achieved (habitualizing a lot of legitimate – authorized – violence under the mask of 'functional' coercion and routinizing it to the point of invisibility), and what its potentially morbid consequences for morality were (substitution of conformity to the rule for responsibility for the Other). I wish I could be similarly sure when taking a stock of 'postmodern' ethics, still *in statu nascendi*, much too new to produce any reliable stochastic chains and risk far-reaching extrapolations from its brief history.

I am not in a better position now than I was ten years ago, working on *Postmodern Ethics*, to commit myself to any verdict with a pretence to finality. Like then, so now, I am inclined to speak about the postmodern moral scene as full of threats and promises, dangers as well as chances. I guess there is hardly anything peculiarly postmodern in being so ambiguous. No perfect setting for moral selves has been found anywhere yet, and all the 'really existing' settings were mixtures of bright auguries and dark premonitions. More importantly, every choice has a price attached and what we gain in one respect we are bound to lose in another. What we see as 'improvements' in the extant setting sooner or later prove to be more or less effective responses to whatever pained us most before, but they bring new (mostly unadumbrated) pains, and so new worries about the sorry state and unprepossessing future of morality. I still think, as before, that the weakening of the ethical codes' grip and the demise of monopolistic ethical authorities and administration centres may in the long run have a beneficial impact on morality; codes used to posit themselves between the moral self and its responsibility. From behind the code the face of the Other was not clearly enough visible, and the moral impulse was all too often used up in the effort of conforming to the code, stopping short of confrontation with the issue of the self's unconditional, and inalienable, responsibility. In the long run it may prove fortunate that the wall of 'responsibility *to*' behind which the moral 'responsibility *for*' was hidden has fallen apart, or that there are too many walls for any of them to offer a secure enough hiding place. There is no guarantee, though, that this is indeed what will happen; not even the probability of its happening is necessarily superior to that of its alternatives.

The codes might have lost much of their morally disabling capacity, but they would not lose it if not for a coincidence of other departures whose disabling capacity might prove no smaller, if not greater, than that of the demand of conformity. We discussed a moment ago one of such departures, the fragmentation, episodicity of life, and the ascendance of *disengagement* to that pivotal point in 'rational' life strategies which used to be occupied by its opposite: engagement and commitment. We have discussed also the new tendency to seek security in a profusion of alternative, but also invariably transient, opportunities rather than in the durability of a setting. You yourself in *Moral Culture* discussed (and worried about) one more fateful departure: the specialization, professionalization, and in the last account commercialization of charity; the new proximity of suffering offered by the worldwide media offers as well a new chance of manipulating and channelling the moral impulses aroused by that 'virtual' proximity. In an essay on 'The Wars of the Globalization Era' I suggest as well that the new 'virtuality' of a category of wars-turned-punitive-expeditions opens quite new vistas for 'adiaphorized' (morally neutralized) cruelty. The point is that all these departures are hardly matters of a freely chosen cultural style: they are, rather, responses which have been and continue to be forced out from the actors by the changed conditions in which we are all obliged to pursue our life tasks. If the rules and stakes of the game change, one could only expect 'sound-minded' players to seek new tactics and make new kinds of moves.

You may say that life lived as a series of self-enclosed episodes and the resulting fluidity of interhuman bonds (presumed even if not genuine) portend hard times for the moral self and the ethical standards of society. It seems to me that there is a close link between the value of durability and the entrenchment of moral standards. It is beneficial for the ethical quality of human intercourse to be aware that 'we will meet again', that we will go on meeting for a long time to come. On the other hand, a tendency to close chapters and to end episodes with a '*not* to be continued' note are linked to the shedding or terminating (perhaps even not undertaking in the first place) of responsibility, that cornerstone of all moral selves. But durability is no longer held in high esteem or seen as a useful quality.

Transience has replaced durability at the top of the value table. What is valued today (by choice as much as by unchosen necessity) is the ability to be on the move, to travel light and at short notice. Power is measured by the speed with which responsibilities can be escaped. Who accelerates, wins; who stays put, loses. Warhol's collection of blatantly, unashamedly non-durable bric-à-brac, appropriated at random, each object purchased on the spur of the moment, not to satisfy a desire even, but to give vent to a momentary wish, and immediately afterwards put on a shelf rather than savoured, or Bill Gates's love for getting rid of things cherished a moment ago, so poignantly observed and so vividly described by Richard Sennett, may serve as paragons of the new cultural ethos. Attachment to objects with a long life expectation goes against the precept to stay slim, light and fit. But that precept, in its turn, militates against taking up moral responsibilities, which may lead to commitments, obligations and other 'burdens' which would be rather, with the rest of the ballast, thrown overboard from the hot-air balloon. All this does not augur well for the recognition of humanity in the Other.

Arts, as always in history, are prompt to symbolically reflect the experience of life in the form they take and the media they use if not in their outspoken, spelled-out message. Happenings and installations meant to last no longer than their fixed-term exhibition are in the forefront of artistic fashion. Works of art (or should one rather talk of art events?) are public rehearsals of the transience of things, of the substitution of experience for what is being experienced. And then comes Damien Hirst, sinking rashers of dead flesh in formaldehyde to inform us of the inanity of dreams of making the transient durable.

A couple of years ago, to talk about postmodernity would have been a very pertinent thing to do, but since the mid-1990s there has been a movement in social thought away from a focus on postmodernity. And it is quite clear that the frequency of appearance of postmodernity in your own work has declined. You have stopped talking about postmodernity and are much more inclined to talk instead about liquid modernity. Why has this shift happened in your work? Is liquid modernity instead of, as well as, or in parallel to postmodernity?

Yes, you are spot on. Over the years I have grown increasingly uneasy with 'postmodernity' as the 'umbrella term' for the wide range of transformations marking the emergent society, and I would very much like to believe that my unease had nothing to do with the notorious volatility of fashions among the chattering classes, including their social-scientific sector. When I resorted to the concept of postmodernity as an axis around which to arrange all that is novel in present-day social reality, I took a distance from the then widely deployed concept of 'postmodernism'. Unlike 'postmodernism', which, like all 'isms', referred to a programme or an attitude more than to any particular features of the 'world out there', 'postmodernity' I hoped would refer to the quality of a particular type of society, which happened to be ours but unlike that of our fathers. Early on I made the distinction between 'postmodern sociology' and 'sociology of postmodernity' and sincerely hoped that the separation of the two could be established and maintained. It looks now that my hopes were unwarranted. 'Postmodernity' and 'postmodernism' have been hopelessly confused, used in many cases synonymically. The very talk of postmodernity has been taken as a sign of joining the 'postmodernist' camp. I found myself in the company of bedfellows with whom I would rather not share a bed, while all too often ideas were read into my texts which were not mine, but belonged to those I was associated with on the strength of semantic confusion. I began my retreat once I had come to the conclusion that in all probability the battle was lost, and that because of the semantic confusion sensible discussion of contemporary trends under the rubric of 'postmodernity' would be well-nigh impossible.

There was another, more substantive reason to retreat. You may lean over backwards to deny it, to pile up reservations, but nothing doing: the word 'postmodernity' implies the end of modernity, leaving modernity behind, being on the other shore. But this is blatantly untrue. We are as modern as ever, obsessively 'modernizing' everything we can lay our hands on. A quandary, therefore: the same but different, discontinuity in continuity. Anthony Giddens found a way out from the predicament by brandishing the term 'late modernity'. I found it difficult to adopt. I never understood how we know that this modernity here and now is 'late', and how we would go about proving or refuting this. Besides, the idea of 'late modernity' implies the same as the concept of postmodernity: one cannot speak of a 'late' phase of a process unless one assumes that the process has fizzled out and that therefore you can eye the 'whole of it'. Ulrich Beck's 'second modernity' is better, but by itself an empty container inviting all sorts of contents. It says nothing about the difference between the 'second' modernity and the 'first'. George Balandier's *surmodernité* I found more palatable; it is a pity that in English translation it does not sound as well as in the original French version. Hence my own proposition: *liquid modernity* which points to what is continuous (melting, disembedding) and discontinuous (no solidification of the melted, no re-embedding) alike. So far, I have found the concept suitable and useful. In the book under the same title I tried to go one by one through some central and very much alive issues which have been put on the social agenda in modern times, in order to find out what has been changed and what has remained unscathed because of the advent of the 'liquid' phase, and it seems to me that the concept helps to 'make sense' of the changes as well as of the continuities.

Conversation 4

Individualization and Consumer Society

KEITH TESTER   *The status of the 'individual' in your social thought is often debated. The individual is an ethical subject, social actor and also the product of specific life strategies. But many people reject the usefulness of talk about the 'individual' because it is too abstract and ignores the social aspects of our identity. What is your attitude to this issue?*

ZYGMUNT BAUMAN   Well, yes, 'individual' is a problematic, trouble-inviting concept, but no more, though no less either, than so many other terms with which the sociological narratives, or for that matter the narratives of our life experience, are composed. And yes, we will probably go on quarrelling about the truth of 'individuality' no end, and whatever we say will be challenged, and both what we say and the rejoinders to it will more often than not have their good reasons. Leibniz used to entertain ladies of the court by sending them to a leafy autumn garden, having told them to find two leaves which were in all respects identical. They failed, of course, and having failed lost their tongue: they were no longer sure that it made sense to speak of 'oak leaves', of 'maple leaves', of 'beech leaves' or 'chestnut leaves', and having lost the confidence that dies the moment reflection is born, they could not speak. A few centuries later Wittgenstein picked the example of 'game' and a collective portrait of the Churchill family to argue that 'family resemblance' does not mean that there is a single feature which all members of the family share. Both Leibniz and Wittgenstein brought into relief, in vivid forms, what had already been vented through centuries before in the never fully resolved dispute between the 'nominalists' and the 'universalists'.

There is no denying that this selective eye-opening and eye-closing, and the undue simplification and impoverishment of reality which the coining of 'collective terms', that is terms which count for more than one unit in the sets they denote, is a problem and a serious challenge for philosophers, logicians or linguists. As to the rest of us though, few if any go through the agony of the kind described in Jean-Paul Sartre's *Nausea*. By and large, all its logical aporias and empirical traps notwithstanding, our language serves our daily tasks quite well, and but seldom have we an occasion to reflect on the mysterious ways in which this awesome feat is daily, ever again, achieved. I propose therefore that we leave this problem to the worry of the professional students of paradoxes and focus instead on another aspect of the issue you've raised, the aspect which has been our, the sociologists', proper domain since the inception of modern social thought: that of the relation between 'individuality' and society, which, in a nutshell, is one more facet of the complex relation between biography and history.

When John Thompson suggested that I collect in one volume scattered articles I have written and lectures I have given in recent years (at the time that I was working on *In Search of Politics* and *Liquid Modernity*), one thing we had to discuss at length was the choice of a title that would best express the connecting idea of the collection. We settled for John's suggestion of *Individualized Society*, but we both regretted that the title most fitting the content of the volume had been already 'taken' by Norbert Elias . . . *Society of Individuals*. Elias's felicitous phrase is spot-on and cannot be bettered, whenever the issue of individuality is explored and narrated. It casts aside both Hobbes's and Spencer's problems which kept several generations of social thinkers busy while prompting them to look in the wrong direction.

Instead it brings into the centre of attention the fact that 'society' is what makes (or does not, as the case may be) the humans into *individuals*, rather than being a miraculous antidote to the terminal poison of immaculately conceived or 'natural' and inborn individuality as Hobbes would have it, or the individual's mortal enemy, as Spencer would insist. Indeed, what we call 'society' is responsible for whether we are viewed as predominantly idiosyncratic or serial entities and whether we subordinate our life strategy (consciously or not) to asserting and cultivating idiosyncrasy or 'conforming to the kind'. And, funnily enough (or not that funny after all, given how common are the imitations of the owl of Minerva's habits), to say 'society' and 'think society' one already needs to be fairly advanced on the road to individuality, know the 'being orphaned' feeling, deprived of guides and wardens and left with the vexingly inadequate maps in the pocket and tools in the private toolbox.

The implication of your answer is that talk about the 'individual' represents an abstraction from interconnectedness and social relationships. In other words, it is not that individuals exist in society but, rather, that society is associated with forms of individuality. That way of dealing with the issue means that it is first of all necessary to be able to talk about society. What is society?

Few of our contemporaries remember that when it first appeared in the language of the emerging science of sociology, 'society' was a metaphor, like all metaphors selective, laying bare certain features of the object to which it was applied while assigning lesser importance to its other traits. From that part or aspect of the world which the sociologists set themselves to explore, the metaphor of society drew to the surface and made salient the quality of being in a 'company'.

Explicitly or implicitly, the metaphor of society uses images of closeness, proximity, togetherness and mutual engagement. 'Society' could be used as a metaphor because the experience which the sociologists struggled to grasp and articulate was that of a number of people sharing the same place, interacting in many if not all of their activities, meeting each other often and talking to each other on many occasions. Being united in such a way, that quantity of people faced the prospect of living in close proximity to each other for a long time to come, and for that reason the unity of the life setting was capped by the effort to close ranks, to make the coexistence 'harmonious', 'orderly', so that 'mutual benefits' might follow.

The paradox, though, is that the kind of experience which sociologists struggled to catch in their conceptual net when using 'society' as a metaphor had become salient because it was already in a state of disrepair and in need of urgent and close attention, requiring new tools for it to be 'caught'. It was precisely the 'company' that was missing, conspicuous for its absence. The experience of 'being in company' had become rare. Not that human settlements had been depopulated and crowds were nowhere to be seen (on the contrary, seldom if ever in the past were streets as densely packed as in the cities sprouting and swelling all over the place) but somehow being in that urban crowd felt different from 'being *in company*', hence by contrast it made visible what 'being in company' was truly about (about 'moral density', as Durkheim would much later suggest, as distinct from 'physical density'). By choosing to apply the metaphor of 'society', sociologists tried to show that these anonymous and faceless crowds that gatecrashed into daily life, and all the rest of people who stayed permanently out of sight, unknown and only known (or heard) of, distant yet somehow interfering, were despite appearances 'like' that company one used to be in; that not all proximity might feel like being in company, but being in company does not require proximity as its necessary condition. Durkheim dedicated his life work to the effort of showing how the effects of streamlining and taming the potentially savage beings can be achieved at a distance, without face-to-face contact, through division of labour and a system of duly modified, yet abstract, law, and achieved as well as when the same effects were attained by communal rituals and close and constant neighbourhood watch.

Does it therefore follow that society was imagined rather than found? And, if that is the case, what were the circumstances of that imagination?

Benedict Anderson encapsulated two centuries of the sociologists' efforts when he coined the concept of 'imagined community'.

I wonder: could 'society' be *imagined* at all, could it become an 'imagined company', were not daily experience already suggesting something quite different – loneliness, abandonment, absence of company? I believe that society became an object of cognition the moment it started making its members into *individuals*, itself retreating from the realm of the visible (let alone the obvious), from the 'given to hand', and taking a behind-the-scenes position, where it could only be 'imagined' and theorized.

What does that 'making people into individuals' consist of? In loosening the ties that cramped human moves, for sure: in 'emancipation from constraints'. But it consists first and foremost in putting the 'becoming' before the 'being'. An individual is a creature whose plight is the summation, consequence or desert of a life of work. Individuals are what they have *become*, each one of them the result of his or her own choices and pursuits. This causal chain may be a postulate rather than a statement of fact, but truth is not at stake here. 'Making people into individuals' means treating that postulate as the actual 'truth of the matter' and viewing the successes gained and the defeats suffered *as if* that was indeed the case.

In this society of ours, we are all individuals, but for most of us the meaning of 'being individual' stops here: at the sense of *being treated* as a 'self-made man or woman'. The choice is all around, just pick it up and follow what you've chosen. If what you desire eludes you, there must be something wrong with you and you alone. Look around: others are making their choices and get what they want, why do you fail? This does not necessarily mean that if only you tried sufficiently hard you might get rid of everything you do not like in that world of yours, that everything in that world is soft and pliable and ready to be remoulded at wish. What it does mean is that such things as cannot be changed and put in desirable shape by your own effort are not worth your second thought, and being concerned with them would be a sheer waste of your time.

The effort is sufficiently vast to keep you busy all your life! You need to find the best diet-and-exercise regime to keep you slim, agile and fit; you need to discover what sort of sexual identity fits you best and then try, one after another, the available means to make you attractive for the sex of your choice; you need to find out how to make friends and influence people; how to pass an interview with flying colours and how to make other people dependent on you without exposing yourself to the danger of dependency; how to be confident that you can steer things your way and how to have trust in that confidence of yours. A lifelong job, indeed.

No wonder we witness these days a veritable 'counselling boom', with so many experts around peddling their wares and obtrusively offering their services: advice on how to make sure that the choice is right and that a wrong choice has been avoided. Their tunes vary, but one motif is audible in every melody: the buck is on your desk (your kitchen, your bedroom, your jogging track and your credit card). It all boils down to your skill, cunning and resolve. It is your action or inaction that makes all the difference between success and failure, pleasure and unhappiness. Anthony Giddens has coined the 'sequestration' concept: we, the individuals, can 'sequestrate' the experts' arcane knowledge, make it our property and handle it as all property is handled – take it or leave it, cultivate it or throw it away. Giddens sees in this the warrant of our autonomy. We are not the wise guys' puppets, we are free to decide. Maybe. But the other aspect of being granted that 'leave to sequestrate' is allowing the experts to stay out of trouble. If the recipe or the regime does not work, it is again your, their chooser and user's fault; you did not look where you should have or looked not closely enough. The expertise as such emerges from the failed trial unscathed, its authority intact, its image unpolluted. The game of counselling-and-sequestration goes on, spurred by the anxieties of loneliness and inadequacy which the life individually lived cannot but daily generate.

This is the world we live in, and this is where all sociological analysis, for better or worse, has to start its conversation with human experience.

So are you saying that sociological analysis should eschew abstractions and, as it were, 'start from here'?

Starting from here is a matter of the relevance or irrelevance of sociological inquiry for the principal recipients of its services in the individualized world. But 'starting from here' is not enough by itself to fulfil an ethical mission. By itself, 'starting from here' is but being realistic, taking a good inventory of the qualities of human experience and drawing a good map of the field of study; in short, a matter of good sense. Taking an ethical stance calls for one more vital step. To be moral means to be willing and ready to come to help.

The problem that prompts such a next step and makes taking it a *conditio sine qua non* of 'moral sociology' is that the state of being socially cast as individuals bearing undivided responsibility for the effects of their actions (and apprehending their plight as the effect of their actions) does not mean that people so cast, all people so cast or a substantial majority of them, can indeed act on that 'responsibility-by-decree'. The opposite is true. Most of us simply lack the resources which true self-assertion, self-definition and self-determination require. But as if that limitation were not enough, there is a more powerful reason yet for the postulate of fully fledged individuality to hang in thin air as far as many of us (perhaps most of us) are concerned: the roots of whatever troubles us and stands in the way of a dignified and morally satisfying life are stuck well beyond the reach of individual action. These roots are *socially* planted and cultivated and only *collectively* can they be dug up and 'detoxified'. But once set in motion, individualization is self-propelling and self-intensifying; one of its foremost achievements is the undermining of the very possibility of *acting socially*, of questioning society first and then following that critique with a shared social practice.

Sociology 'with a moral conscience' would need to pass another test on top of starting from the recognition that 'we are all individuals now'. It would have to disclose the mechanism of that peculiar individualizing process which happens to be our lot; the mechanism akin to that invented by the Pharaoh who commanded his Hebrew slaves to go on producing bricks but forbade the supply to them of the straw needed for production. It would have to redirect our attention, fully consumed at the moment with self-centred concerns, to the fact that the quality of individually administered life depends on factors which are not individually, but socially managed and that without addressing the issues of that social management not much can be done, certainly not enough, to improve on that quality. In a curious way the meaning of 'moral sociology' has been reversed. It used to be, in times of 'solid modernity', the task of defending individual freedom and dignity against the rising totalitarian tide flowing from concentrated and condensed social powers. It is now, or at least it seems to me to be, the task of reconstituting society as the common property and common responsibility of free individuals aiming at a dignified life.

Leszek Kolakowski offers some resources for a way of thinking about the moral significance of the individual in his little book Freedom, Fame, Lying and Betrayal. *He says that humans are free and able to choose between good and evil; it is that ability to choose that makes people responsible for their actions and, at the same time, worthy of being accorded a certain dignity. Kolakowski suggests that because we are free we possess dignity, and dignity demands to be taken into account, it demands to be respected. What is your assessment of this argument?*

Yes, as it is in his habit, my learned friend Leszek Kolakowski is right beyond doubt: were it not for our freedom of choice, the concept of dignity would have no sense. More than that, though: the concept of dignity would not arise. The kind of imagination that can beget this concept is born in the experience of choosing between good and evil while simultaneously being an object of such choices. But let me add that as in the case of justice, so in the case of dignity. It is the negative experience, in this case the experience of *indignity*, that comes first. Dignity is born in a protest against the ugly and painful contents of experience, as a postulate: the postulate to negate negativity. Such a birth would be unthinkable had we not already been eating from the tree of knowledge of good and evil and were we not already practising the agonizingly difficult art of living with that knowledge. And so you are right as well: freedom and dignity go hand in hand, they are born and they die together. And in as far as the individual is free (or in other words in as far as human freedom takes the form of individuation), individuality joins that indivisible pair to form (let me risk that term) the Human Trinity.

It all hangs, however, on the content of freedom. To be free to choose may mean no more than the absence of powers that prohibit the choice, or powers that use their ability to coerce us to confine our choices to an unduly narrow range they would agree to tolerate. But being free may mean something more than that: the ability of free persons to influence the range of choices at their disposal and to practise the art of choosing between them effectively. What follows from the discussion we had a moment ago is that these two ingredients of freedom may not be simultaneously present and that while having done a lot to supply the first ingredient, our type of society has not done nearly enough to secure the second. This duality would surely extend to the other units of the Trinity, closely dependent, as they are, on the quality of freedom. We have hinted as much in the case of individuality, but something must be said yet about the third element of the Trinity: dignity.

The word 'dignity' has many meanings, reflecting many aspirations, all of them shaped in and by the world their users inhabit. To be denied choice in the world of choosers is indignity. To be denied the right to mobility of one's choice in the world of travellers and tourists is indignity. To be denied the right to put on display one's preferences in the world of 'human rights' and ever expanding tolerance of one's form of life is indignity. But to show one's ineptitude in all such spheres in the world of 'self-made individuals' is also indignity, and arguably the most painful of them all, a sort of 'meta-indignity' in fact. In a world that promotes happiness to the supreme rank among the purposes of life, to have one's access to happiness cut off is indignity; and that indignity is yet more agonizing if the blocking of access is one's own doing, as it surely must be – must it not? – among the self-made individuals. You can learn a lot about the nature of human condition in a given society by collecting current meanings of 'indignity' and finding out which of the meanings is most commonly, and most vociferously, alluded to in human complaints. Accordingly, the meaning of 'dignity' demanded or defended changes from one kind of society to another, and also from one 'social spot' to another.

Each society, I am tempted to say, trims dignity to its own measure. All trimming, though, is already demeaning. As creatures endowed with the wondrous (even if not always pleasurable) ability to choose between good and evil or right and wrong, should not the humans be able to oppose it? Above all, should they not have a say when (if) the cuts are made? In other words: are there not good grounds to postulate a kind of dignity which transcends any of the forms already moulded by any given society, a 'metadignity' so to speak, dignity that consists precisely in making one's voice heard, and listened to, when it comes to deciding what a person wishing dignity should strive for and under what conditions?

We are back to Castoriadis, to his insistence that individuals cannot be autonomous unless society is. And society is not autonomous if (to follow Castoriadis's argumentation and terminology) 'the council and the people' cannot or would not say that this or that law is binding because, and only because, this council and this people here and now think it to be right and to be for the best: if society, instead, accepts that it is pushed and pulled by forces, sighted or blind, which it cannot stand up to and must meekly and placidly obey. Should we not say that living life under the aegis of 'there is no alternative' is an indignity of society, in the same way as having no capacity to choose is the indignity of the individual? Just as with autonomy, so the dignity of the society and that of each of its members are intimately connected, inseparable, and mutually dependent. Dignity of the individuals can be fulfilled only in a dignified society.

One of the main threads in critical social thought is precisely the idea that dignity has been undermined. There is Marx's picture of alienated labour, Weber on the prisoners of the iron cage, Marcuse's one-dimensional man and Mills's 'cheerful robots'. A similar temper can be found in your own work. In the Freedom *book you take one of the most vaunted values of the West (and for that matter one of the most important values in your own thought) and critique what freedom has become and substantially means from the point of view of a set of implicit assumptions about what freedom could be. Throughout, you insist that freedom is analysed as a relationship (one person has freedom because the other does not; the freedom of the former is gained at the expense of the possibility of the freedom of the latter). As such, you put freedom in a thoroughly sociological frame of understanding.*

Our type of society, at least most of the time, tells us to seek, as Beck put it, 'biographical solutions to systemic contradictions' even if the chances of being able to follow the advice of such common sense are slim to say the least, since for most of us such solutions simply do not exist.

And so there is room for suspicion that individuality and individual freedom are a sham: that hidden behind the ostensible 'individualization' a new slavery is taking root; that while people may be indeed seeking their own unique biographical solutions to life problems, their search and most certainly their findings are prescripted, decided in advance so they should all fall into a narrowly circumscribed pattern.

There have been many names under which such a suspicion has been vented. To list but a few: one-dimensional man, 'cheerful robots' which you've mentioned, but also 'other-directed man' of David Riesman and most notably 'mass society' producing 'massmen' on a massive scale, not to speak of the ubiquitous alarms about the innate taints of the 'bourgeois' or the 'embourgeoised', with their inclination to conformity, distaste for originality and inclination to fall in line and 'live up (or down) to the Joneses'.

There were many attempts to explain why this must be so: efforts to raise the described tendencies to the level of necessity determined by the nature of society to which we belong or by the nature of us, who belong to that society. Recall for instance 'the fear of the void' of Adorno and Horkheimer, the 'escape from freedom' of Erich Fromm, Vance Packard's 'hidden persuaders', or go back further still to Gustave LeBon's 'crowd' (later exquisitely elaborated upon by Elias Canetti) or Gabriel Tarde's 'imitation'. The same themes return over and over again in different garbs, updated according to the latest fashion but only slightly modified. The themes fall, roughly, into two categories: either society is blamed for forcing or luring people to copycat, or people themselves are blamed for putting the copycat kind of behaviour above the challenges of self-creation and self-assertion.

There is hardly ever smoke without a fire. Though in the heat of the battle we tend to deny the adversaries their reasons, there is a lot to be said in each opinion's favour. Modern society sets in motion powerful individualizing pressures, but it also erects barriers that make the road to individuality rough, jolting and all too often impassable. Let us not forget, however, that the particular fire which the smoke of the 'mass society' signals is burning in the homes of those who detest 'mass society', finding it unpalatable and contrary to true humanity. They bewail its rising while themselves feeling (hoping to be) immune to its baits, like Odysseus was to the sirens' seductive songs. The 'mass culture' and similar debates say a lot about the plight of 'the people', but they say no less, if not more, about the condition of the polemicists. 'Mass culture' or 'cheerful robots' are the portraits which reveal simultaneously some aspects of the sitters' physique but also the viewpoint of the painters.

However the authors saw the people they described, they looked at them from where they stood, and they could hardly do otherwise. The learned classes of modern times, later to be called 'intellectuals', were from the start 'professional individuals'. Their position and professional roles required originality, experimenting, and questioning or rejection of orthodoxy and its perpetual transcendence; and they had to prove their mettle by demonstrating that they were indeed able to excel in all such endeavours. No wonder that their idea of a 'good society' was of a kind of society which approves of and actively promotes this kind of attitude and behaviour.

By itself, though, this circumstance did not yet determine that the charge of mass behaviour and the refusal of individuality should be raised against the *hoi polloi*, or that a charge of prompting such sins be raised against their rulers and managers. Quite a few among the intellectuals, after all, considered individuality a privilege of the betters, a precious gift not to be squandered and not to be trusted to all the rest who can neither appreciate it nor handle it with care. In *Legislators and Interpreters* I collated a fairly long list of contemptuous and derisive opinions of the 'stupid herd-like mass', 'given to stampede rather than solitary walks', expressed by the greatest minds of the modern era. For the learned classes to bewail the advent of 'mass society', two more conditions must have been met. First, the spiritual

leadership to which the learned classes aspired must have
been pursued through enlightenment rather than coercive
control. Second, that pursuit must have been found vain or
in danger of becoming ineffective due to the unfair competition coming from all sorts of wrong quarters ('mass media',
and writers of commercial copy and their ilk being the prime
villains of the piece), or because of the refusal of the ignorant
to be enlightened, thanks to their revolting propensity to
reject the advice of good taste and their outrageous craving
for 'vulgar' pastimes and inferior cultural products. The
laments against the grass-roots resistance to individuality, or
the tendency at the top to knead the would-be and should-
be individuals into a mass, were, in short, prompted by the
awkward feeling that control over the process is slipping
from the hands of the classes called to preside over it, and
that the 'project of enlightenment' is bound in consequence
to stay 'unfinished' or come to nothing.

The critique of reality is born in the gap between the
'ought' and the 'is'. Since the learned classes of our days
have grown lukewarm to the idea of the 'good society'
together with the ambition of prodding, let alone guiding,
'the people' towards it, one may surmise that the gap in
question has shrunk and so the critique would have run out
of steam. There are indeed signs that this is happening. One
does not hear these days about the horrors of 'mass society'
as often as one did half a century ago. It is rather common
to hear that we are all individuals now and that not much
remains to be done to make us more individual than we are:
with history at its end, let us live happily ever after. One
wonders whether this change of tune has been caused by the
rising of the 'masses' to the level of individuality or by a
lowering of the sights of those who record their progress.

Let me however return to the query you've addressed
directly to me, and particularly to my short essay on *Freedom*. I do touch there (albeit briefly and superficially) on the
ambiguity endemic to the intellectual stance towards the
prospect of universal individuality, but the point you raised,
of freedom being a *social relation*, is only partly related

(though, I agree, not entirely unrelated) to this problem. What I argued in that essay was something else, a fairly obvious point, come to think of it: since the ability to get things to turn as one wishes them to turn is the innermost essence of the experience of freedom, and since achieving this effect depends inevitably on other people abiding by our wishes even if our wishes clash with their own, then freedom is, potentially, a zero-sum game, that is a game in which the gain of some players is a loss of some others. In that game there cannot be winners without losers. The freedom of some entails the unfreedom of some others. If this is so, freedom (at any rate the positive freedom, the capacity of doing things) tends to be a privilege rather than a universal and equally shared possession. I repeat: this point seems to be pretty obvious, and yet it happens to be absent in the debates about freedom which tend to evolve around the abstract 'individual as such'. Recognizing the truth of that point is further hampered by the fact that as a rule the *haute couture* specimens of freedom at the top are fast followed by the mass-production copies for the 'ordinary folk', inferior, fraudulent copies to be sure. Freedom seems to be as common a possession as refrigerators, and yet all too often the hapless customers of the freedom supermarkets, lumbered with mass-production copies of the real thing, wonder what those crazies up there make such a fuss about and why.

The Freedom *book raises the issue of consumerism and the consumer society. Now, whenever you discuss consumer society your tone always betrays the presence of a deep and committed critique. You refuse to accept consumerism on its own terms. What are the key strands of your critique of consumerism?*

Being saddled with the task of finding biographical solutions to systemic contradictions is an unprepossessing condition to be in, and the all-too-natural, widely shared wish to escape it is the principal stuff of which the market's seductive baits are forged; markets seem to allure their prospective customers to use their freedom of choice to obtain patented cures for the unpleasant side-effects of that freedom.

I would say that the most pernicious impact of the consumer market is the promise that a cure for all the troubles you may suffer is waiting somewhere in some shop and can be found if you search earnestly enough. The after-effects of that promise are threefold, each one of the three deadly. One is 'social deskilling', a neglect to learn the skills of discussing and negotiating the ways out of trouble with others, and the belief that such skills are not really necessary, since the solution to the problem can be obtained with less effort and at a smaller price during the next shopping escapade. Another is the conclusion that dealing with life problems is, like the intake of consumables, a solitary affair which cannot gain much in effectiveness from being conducted in cooperation with others. The third effect consists in, so to speak, substituting the fight against symptoms for the healing of the disease: however keen and astute a shopper you may be, you will not find in the shops a remedy for the social causes of your troubles, only the recipe for how to mollify the trials and tribulations caused (or simply to forget the trouble for the duration of chasing the recipes and the attached gadgets). The rise of the consumer is the fall of the citizen. The more skilful the consumer, the more inept the citizen. This is, roughly, my reply to what you've asked me about, 'the key strands of my critique of consumerism'.

Each social incarnation has its own standards of dignity; so does the reincarnation of the citizen (as well as of the producer, of 'the doer of things') into a consumer. I remember my mother being proud of her washing skills when relishing the impeccable whiteness of the bed linen which she rubbed against the washboard, soaked, ran through the mangle and ironed. The present-day mother (or father) would take pride in locating the supermarket shelf with the best brand of washing powder and purchasing a particularly skilful washing machine. Both claimed dignity for what they were proud of. Would you, in clear conscience, refuse to grant it to either of them? The strength of consumerism lies in its coming complete with its very own outlet for the 'instinct of workmanship', its own standards of propriety and, indeed, of dignity. These standards can be starkly different from the kind of standards you would wish to prevail in their stead, but don't hold your disaffection against the millions who gladly dispose of the washboards once the washing machine is on offer.

Consumerism is a form of life. There have been, are and will be other forms, and each has its attractions and its off-putting aspects, different in each case. Let us concentrate on the demerits of the consumer form of life, its dangers, its deprivations, and try to remedy or attenuate them, if we can. Let us alert ourselves and others to what we all miss knowingly or unknowingly, like the joys of the social or moral economies which the market economy would not nor can offer. Let us hammer home the truth that consumerism is not a 'there is no alternative' predicament, but a choice (though a choice by default rather than design, and a choice made collectively, though by a 'collectivity' which can be only 'imagined'), and let us ensure that whatever choice is made will be a conscious and a fully considered one. But let us accept as well that struggling to stay in the consumer game is, in this world of ours, a way to pursue the eternal human dream of dignity. One cannot be blamed for the conditions. If one can be blamed at all, it is for not counting the losses which these conditions inflict when their blessings are counted or thoughtlessly enjoyed.

Not everyone can possess the dignity which is implied and promoted by consumer society. After all, if I am going to be a consumer who is able to make choices, I need money and certain skills. But money and consumer skills go together – not everyone has enough money to be accorded the dignity of being a competent consumer and neither, therefore, do they possess the kinds of competence that the consumer society rewards. They are, as you have often said, 'flawed consumers'. But if there is a divide between the able and the flawed consumers, do they thus come to live in very different moral universes with high walls keeping them apart?

We all live in a society of consumers, and we cannot – at least singly or severally – help it. Living in the society of consumers means to be measured, evaluated, praised or denigrated by the standards appropriate to consumer life. Those who for whatever reason cannot play the game properly would be (in their own eyes as much as in the eyes of others) denied dignity and thus humiliated on top of all the other sufferings, bodily or spiritual, which they may be forced to bear. One's astuteness in a consumer world depends on the volume of resources one can muster and deploy; those who can muster and deploy but little are defective, blemished or flawed consumers. They don't pass the test of dignity.

You may ask: were not the poor 'flawed' as well in the society of producers? Since other things were foremost on human minds then, they were flawed *producers* (they did not contribute much to the wealth of the nation when that wealth was measured by the amount of labour rather than the volume of consumption) but *flawed* all the same. Yes, this is true, but being flawed as producers or as consumers has a different impact on human dignity. I remember Margaret Thatcher retorting to the suggestion that rising unemployment had something to do with rising crime: How dare you insinuate such a thing! Our unemployed are nice and gentle people, they would not steal! Who – including Margaret Thatcher – would say the same about the 'underclasses' of the consumer society?! For the presence of 'flawed producers' society stood accused and it was society – 'the strength and the wealth of the nation' – that was feared to be suffering when the number of the 'flawed' grew. Investing in the readiness of the unemployed for redeployment once better times returned meant investing in everybody's future well-being. Keynes's idea of beefing up consumer demand to stimulate production sounded convincing in the society of producers, but it has been duly dropped at the entry to the consumer society. Investing in the poor in a society of consumers may be a *morally* correct act, but it conspicuously has no *economic* sense. It won't add to anybody else's well-being either, since it would leave 'less money in the consumer's pocket' and push up the prices of goods and services. As to the recipients of help, all assistance offered would be seen as, purely and simply, an act of charity; a feather in the donors' caps, but another item in the long list of the receivers' indignities. So in what kind of merits, present or future, can the 'flawed consumers' seek a saving grace? There seem to be no grounds on which they could claim dignity. And the dignity tends to be, summarily, refused to the 'underclass' which they have now become. Moreover, the condemnation tends to be accepted by the condemned.

In his series of penetrating studies of the ghetto and the 'mean streets' or 'rough estate' dwellers, Loïc Wacquant invariably found the same stories of self-contempt and self-derision told over and over again by his respondents [see, for example, Bourdieu et al. 1999]. The people 'down there' (that is, on their home ground) are good for nothing, they say. Today's poor feel no solidarity with each other's lot. They may like and keep company with some of their fellows-in-fate, they may fear them or admire their prowess, but they would hardly respect them. They would deny their dignity no less eagerly than do the people who keep clear of the 'no go areas'. How different it is from the attitudes recorded in the districts afflicted by mass unemployment in the times of economic depression, among the residents who could say in clear conscience that their blight came from the absence of the jobs which would offer them their share in human dignity. In the Great Depression of the thirties visitors to the working-class quarters were astonished to find the unemployed busy day in day out, doing small jobs around the house, repairing roofs and fixing wobbly table legs, and their wives scrubbing the floors already shining from constant scrubbing and washing the shirts already threadbare from constant washing. The business of dignified working-class life went on as usual, with yet more hard effort and dedication than usual. Powder was kept dry, self-respect and the right to be respected kept alive through the times of trial.

You suggest that the successful and the defeated, the heroes of the consumer society and those humiliated by it, 'live in different moral universes'. I would not accept this. I would rather agree with Jeremy Seabrook's reminders that the poor live in a world dominated by the triumphant standards of the rich and that this circumstance, if anything, adds insult to injury (remember also Richard Sennett's disclosure of the 'hidden injuries of class'), while depriving the poor of the little chance they could have of coming clean of either. Atomized and quarrelsome, mutually despising 'flawed consumers', what can they possibly dream of? Of becoming rich and so earning the dignity owed solely to the flawless consumers. The rich are not enemies, but examples. Not hate figures, but idols.

And the life the idols teach, the example they set to be followed by the rest, are for the outcasts of consumer society anything but uplifting. No longer the moral tales of a shoeshine boy turning into a millionaire through hard work, parsimony and self-denial. An altogether different fairy-tale instead, of chasing moments of ecstasy, spending lavishly and stumbling from one stroke of luck to another, with both luck and misadventure being accidental and inexplicable and but tenuously related to what the lucky and the unlucky did, and seeking luck, as one seeks a winning lottery ticket, in order to chase more fun and have more moments of ecstasy and spend more lavishly than before. And above all: the sight of corruption, of grabbing chances when they come, of unearned earnings, unpaid taxes, golden hand-shakes for botched jobs. None of the examples that descend from the top can show those at the bottom how to cope with the challenges of their own condition, but all of them together divert from doing anything effective about it. When reflected in the distorting mirror of poverty, the 'dignity of the rich' rebounds as the indignity of the underclass.

And so I would say: it is a pity, and the bottom half's misfortune, that the two parts of our increasingly polarized society *do not* live 'in different moral universes'.

How is it possible to achieve a sense of individual solidity and authenticity in consumer society if everything to hand is transient?

'Authenticity' is not a vernacular term. More importantly yet, the contents inscribed into that term in learned debates do not seem to be drawn from commonly shared experience. The home ground of 'authenticity' is the discourse of (to use Luc Boltanski and Eva Chiapello's concept) the 'artistic critique' which is aimed against homogenizing pressures exerted by modern society and its endemic conformity, the fear of 'standing out', marking 'bourgeois culture'. This is a discourse confined by and large to a relatively narrow sector of the learned classes, mostly artists and poets, the pioneers of individuality, the first people to be cast in a situation of obligatory self-constitution and burdened with the task of conjuring up their own uniqueness. 'Artistic critique' was born, as Boltanski and Chiapello point out, of 'the tension between the mobility of the artist and the obsessive fixity of those who prospered in the world of business'. Remember that the time they refer to was one of 'solid modernity', 'heavy capitalism', 'big is beautiful' and 'engagement on the ground'; the tycoons of heavy capitalism were indeed 'fixed to the ground', defined in no uncertain manner by their all-too-material and immovable possessions. In that world in which 'holding to the ground' (that is, *grounded* wealth) was the sign of distinction and the precept of a successful life, the artists were among the first to have their anchors cut and to be set afloat, and the first to try the recasting of that fate into a vocation, and of the vocation into the sign of superiority and entitlement to privilege. This was not a mean task, considering that by the opinion prevailing in the world of 'solid modernity', mobility as a lifestyle, lack of a fixed address and the resulting state of being 'underdefined', as most artists and poets used to be most of the time, were viewed as symptoms of mindlessness, shiftiness, dangerous recklessness and unforgivable frivolity, unreliability and moral depravation. 'Authenticity' was born as a part of the 'black is beautiful' type of response; an attempt to turn the stigma of shame into a badge of honour.

'Authenticity' originated as a clarion call, a war-cry. Let it now be the turn of those who placidly wear the officially certified masks while being careful not to show any part of their real face (if they still have any), those who exchange their selves (or whatever is left of them) for a bunch of officially assigned roles while being careful not to deviate from the script and not make audible their own voice (if such a voice still remains), to feel ashamed of themselves and feel the need to apologize, if not to reform their ways. Whoever wears masks and plays roles lives a lie. The truth is hidden inside, struggling to get out; let each individual be a midwife of her or his self – *l'ipseite*, the unique self, unrepeatable, unlike any other, non-exchangeable for any other.

'Authenticity' has been throughout a word of an agonistic language, serving the battle for authority. Wherein lies the prerogative to decide between right and wrong? In the standards prevailing 'out there' of which the appointed courts are the guardians, or 'in here', the land impenetrable to intruders and known solely to its rightful individual owner, the sole person entitled to decide and pass judgement on the propriety of the decision? That the artistic critics of the *bourgeois philistines* were up in arms to promote the second alternative, no wonder. Their life experience amply corroborated the choice. When in perpetual movement, the self seems to be the only constant and stable point (in a rotating sphere only the axis does not move); it is the rest of the world which is fickle, forever a-changing, protean and, indeed, stubbornly and unstoppably on the move. The truth is that when recounting their own experience, the critics anticipated the sensations which their antagonists, for a time unable to comprehend, let alone to approve of the story, were yet to taste, and on a massive scale. The irony of that truth is that its verification has eventually been achieved not by pushing away the lid suppressing the repressed authenticity of the self, but as a consequence of the bottom falling out of the 'inner truth' container.

I surmise that the war of authenticity is over by now. The war of words has all but faded away: business managers and artists, office employees and travelling pop stars partake of the same experience of the world-on-the-move and none of them can sensibly seek solid ground and continuity anywhere except in their own body and hopefully (though with much less certainty) in their own self (personality, identity, character, or whatever other names it is called). Stockbrokers and salespeople floating in cyberspace flock to weekend seminars to meet the experts in meditation, not in 'scientific management', and to let loose their inner forces, not learn the ways of taming or defusing them. So there is no more need to quarrel. The former antagonists understand each other perfectly well. Besides, with the hole gaping in that once solid container hoped to contain the self, both sides of the fizzling-out war have other troubles to consume their attention.

I suppose that it is not the desire to 'be authentic' that lies heavily on their mind, but the fear of being 'too authentic', too authentically authentic, of discovering that solid core inside that would not budge or be moved and would thereby set an unencroachable limit to the flexibility of the self. Having ceased to be a weapon in authority wars, the postulate of authenticity has lost much of its past attraction, while its previously not evident, but less prepossessing (and less convenient), facets came to the surface. From an asset, 'authenticity' turns into liability.

It follows from its definition that authenticity, like truth, may be only one: you cannot be 'authentic' all the time you are taking on and dropping off many and different shapes and colours, unless it is the *absence* of authenticity which is one's distinctive (distinctive, indeed?) mark. And it is such 'authenticity' – the absence of commitment and particularly a lasting commitment to any particular form, opening to the (by definition surprising) future, facility in changing 'identity' frequently and without delay when opportunity knocks – that is thought to be the most profitable asset, and which for this reason tends to become a most coveted value. Woe to all who can be 'authentic' in only one, non-negotiable way. The good life (a life least vulnerable) is one of experimenting and new beginnings. People who enter our kind of world are notorious for delaying as long as possible all forms of engagement: to the kinds of study they would like to follow (while avoiding such as lead to narrowly circumscribed specialities), to the kind of job they would like to perform and the company they would like to work for, to the partner in marriage, to the family yet to be started – all such steps which once were seen as necessary on the road to authenticity.

Writing up the analytical history of the era which I call 'solid modernity', Alain Peyrefitte came to the conclusion that its dynamism, and the thorough rehashing and overhauling job it performed on the society it inherited, would have been inconceivable without three kinds of trust most actors had: in oneself, in the others, and in the social institutions. The last one was perhaps the most crucial: it offered a lasting frame in which the much shorter lifespan of individual actors and their intercourses could be inscribed, to which it could be referred and against which it could be evaluated. In all three of its varieties 'trust' could be grounded in the reasonable expectation of longevity and the irrevocability of commitments. What Peyrefitte suggests is that there is no real confidence (or self-confidence for that matter) without the 'longterm' and its institutional embodiments. The wobbliness and 'until-further-noticeness' of social institutions triggers the implosion of confidence in all its varieties. When this leg shakes, the whole tripod promptly collapses.

By the way, perhaps no one explored the dilemma of the self's 'hard core' better than Henrik Ibsen in the adventures of Peer Gynt. His hero found out – the hard way – that his 'authentic self' could be neither invented nor discovered. The invented one appeared to be met with miscomprehension and resentment. The effort of discovery – stripping one by one the roles played in public – led, like stripping the successive layers of an onion, to the nothingness in that centre where hard stone was hoped to be found. Peer Gynt in the end came across a solution to his quandary: love, which was there from the beginning, waiting for his return from the expeditions doomed to fail. In their union and mutual commitments two separate beings found their authenticity. This seems to be indeed the answer, but the question to which this is the answer is ever more seldom asked.

Presumably what some analysts call 'pure relationships' would be identified by you as part of the problem of individualization, not part of the answer?

A 'pure relationship' (that is, ultimately, a relationship assumed by each partner to last as long as, but not a minute longer than, the satisfaction she or he derives) puts paid to the only answer to the authenticity query which Peer Gynt found effective. Relationship (more generally: commitment) offers support in the individual's trials and tribulations when it is understood that its life expectation reaches beyond the lifespan of the lonely warriors and their troubles, that it will survive their defeats as much as it survives their triumphs (for richer and poorer, in health and sickness, the formula goes). Brittle and admittedly short-lived relationships do not meet the bill. On the contrary, they become liabilities cramping future movements. But relationships are brittle and friable precisely because of their purity. We usually, and wisely, tie many times over, with several strings, a parcel which we do not want to fall apart. There must be more ties, and of a different sort, than notoriously erratic satisfaction for the relationship to be of benefit when harsh life tests are individually faced.

Ironically, as the bonds weaken and relationships grow

tenuous, 'connectedness' becomes a widely cherished quality and a trait avidly sought by the employers in their prospective employees. 'Being well connected, having many connections' turns out to be a most reliable warrant of upward mobility. But it is not the strength, but the number of connections, not the durability, but the easiness of entering them (and by implication abandoning them), that counts. As in so many other areas, quantity deputizes for quality. When none of the items in the collection is truly reliable one can count only on their excess and ever growing supply. The wider the network, the better. Never mind the short lifespan of every connecting cable.

There are some nice comments in Liquid Modernity *where you talk about the contemporary cult of the public confessional in a certain genre of television programmes. Are individuals now fated to live their lives in the full glare of publicity? Has privacy been crushed in our kind of social life?*

Long ago Richard Sennett coined the term 'destructive Gemeinschaft'; a community systematically destroyed and methodically destroying its members through the cult of unrestrained sincerity, surrender of one's own privacy and disregard for the privacy of others, confiding the feelings that are and should stay intimate, and demanding that candidness is reciprocated (an act that can only embarrass the partners and cast them in an unbearably awkward position). Sennett discussed the birth of destructive Gemeinschaft in the context of the 'fall of public man', sensing in its appearance one of the greatest dangers that the art of public life faces. 'Public life' is a game with rules, and the most crucial rule is the observance of a certain etiquette which allows us to share what can and ought to be shared by keeping the sentiments, the *Erlebnisse* which cannot be shared, in private reserve. Breaking that rule would prompt the partners to shift away, Sennett warned. It would increase distance instead of making proximity closer, and in the end make true togetherness impossible.

In the picture Sennett painted it was one person in the group who volunteered to wear his heart on his sleeve, to 'open up', to take off all brakes on sincerity and go the whole hog in his confession, forcing the others against their wishes to listen and approve. Sennett's dark premonition was recorded three decades ago. Little could the author then know of the *group* forcing its members into public confessions, demanding them to share publicly their secrets, and claiming that sharing in such secrets is the group's right.

Alain Ehrenberg located the birth of such self-destructive Gemeinschaft in France on one autumn evening in 1983 when, sitting in the full glare of TV cameras, a certain Vivianne informed millions of viewers that her husband Michel was afflicted with premature ejaculation and therefore she had never experienced orgasm in her marital bed. Since then public confessions on innumerable chat-shows have become daily nourishment of the souls famished for company. In glaring contradiction to Sennett's diagnosis, we are daily told, as authoritatively as it could be told in the age of mass media, that we could and we should build community around the confessional, where we are all meant to confess while playing the confessor's role.

There is no room left for the suspicion that respect for the Other may require sparing her or him the embarrassment of witnessing someone else's dirty or not, indecent or not, but as a rule unsightly and nerve-straining, secrets.

A no mean feat accomplished by the confessional society is the conducting of the destruction of individual autonomy under the banner of its self-assertion. This is what the identification of community with making that disclosure into a public spectacle amounts to. The effect advertised and extolled as the triumph of individuality amounts in practice to an escape from the pains and torments, but also the challenges and opportunities, of individuality. 'Individuality' boils down to handling *individually what everyone else* is busy handling, and reporting the experience in words easily understood, since spoken by everyone else. Ultimately, 'individuality' is sought through the smothering of privately groomed idiosyncrasy.

Occasionally, but frequently enough, the laborious process of the dissolution of individuality, in the public ritual of exhibiting the photocopies of approved individual emotions, is short-circuited in the widely publicized public festivals of individual emotions. The sudden death of a celebrated princess, the carefully orchestrated celebration of the first showing of a film earmarked for breaking box-office records, the eagerly awaited midnight when another instalment of a cult story goes on sale, all these and similar events supply the occasion to let out one's individual 'deep emotions' while being reassured that they are indeed individual since all other certified individuals in sight display them.

In these circumstances, about what, then, might the individual hope? Presumably we cannot hope even for a happy death. After all, who or what is going to make our death inhere in memory, who or what is actually going to care?

Your question could make many people pause and worry, if not for the fact that concern with the durability of anything except bodily life is fading fast and the quality of 'lasting' is daily losing its value at the stock exchanges of human happiness. To the best of my knowledge, the sole commodity advertised for its indestructibility in recent years was the video cassette; but its eternal life was alluring thanks to the implied promise that the user will be able to go on endlessly effacing the recorded past and start recording from scratch. In our 'casino culture', as George Steiner famously dubbed the lifestyle cultivated by the consumer market, a happy life is one perceived as the perpetuity of new beginnings. Immortality, like everything else, must be user-friendly and precooked for instant consumption; and what one craves is the *experience* of immortality, not the real thing, obscure, full of traps and labour intensive as it is. What we crave, and what we get, is a world as a theme park of infinity;

infinity of space, of time, but first and foremost of the yet-untried sensations.

What we witness these days is immortality itself becoming mortal. But mortality stops being worrying if it comes together with the promise of raising the dead. The dread of death used to be brought home by the realization that one has but one life to live and that a chance missed is a chance that cannot be recovered. But that truth is belied now by the offer to squeeze as many 'new and improved' lives into the lifespan as one can manage, and the advice that the quicker the successive lives are removed and replaced, the more of them will be packed in and so the volume of 'immortal experiences' will swell. This is, if you wish, but another instance of the wide rule which we briefly touched on before: the excess of offers compensating for the poor quality of every one among them, but also for the benchmark against which that quality could be assessed but which is now no longer on offer.

Try, try, and try again, perhaps next time lucky, but being able to go on trying is the greatest luck that may come your way. The prospect of ever coming to a stop and being saddled once and for all with what has already been around is truly off-putting, the most odious misfortune that may befall you. Things are obtained to be consumed, not kept. They are not expected nor desired to last, lest they clutter the site where other 'new and improved' things could be enjoyed. As in Leonia, one of Italo Calvino's *Invisible Cities*, good luck and happiness are measured by the amount of waste you can dump with no regret.

To cut a long story short: duration has been devalued, while the value of transience is rapidly climbing. We have not been in this condition yet and we can hardly begin to see through its consequences, let alone *long-term* consequences. Human culture was always and in all its forms an ingenious contraption for erecting lasting edifices, using admittedly friable and short-lived materials, or for straining solid crystals of eternity out of the fluid of mortal moments. This was culture's forever inconclusive task, but its sheer inconclusiveness has been culture's power, the paramount source of its inventiveness and never exhausted energy. Now however the task itself seems to be taken off the agenda. It is now the turn of the admittedly temporary bodily life to tower with all the grandeur of eternal rock above the whirlwind of transitory and death-bound objects of desire, jobs, skills, partnerships, pleasures, lifestyles, life purposes and life dreams.

I repeat: we have not been here before, so we do not really know what to expect. Futurology, always a suspect pastime, has become more risky than ever before, and more fraudulent than ever before in case its practitioners deny it. And I repeat after you: 'who and what is actually going to care?' This is the question.

Conversation 5

Politics

KEITH TESTER   *In the second conversation you said that you understand the emergence of a concern with politics in your work as a 'follow-up on Levinasian ethics'. You explained that 'the problem of extending moral insights and impulses to society at large . . . is a matter of politics.' But the move from ethics to politics is not one which Levinas's work necessarily implies. Rather Levinas's ethics points directly in the direction of theology (as an example: it is possible to find John Paul II citing Levinas in an approving way).*

In Levinas the face of the Other is an ethical demand because it can express suffering and, importantly, because it is a transcendence of totality. Levinas says that the face of the Other bears a resemblance to the face of God although it is not identical to God. In this way, Levinas draws a distinction between the particular face and the infinity of God. This is a dominant theme in Levinas's ethics and it is the meaning of the infinity of the ethical demand upon which he focuses. By this line then, Levinas raises the question of the relationship of ethics with theology. It can be argued that Levinas shatters the kind of secular thought that is represented and expressed by sociology. He cannot be contained within it at all.

But your reading of Levinas has always been steadfastly secular; the 'God bit' is noticeably absent. It might be proposed that it is only because of your thoroughly secular (secularized and secularizing) reading of Levinas that the emergence of a problem of politics comes to be obvious.

Your reading of Levinas is made all the more interesting if attention is paid to your own texts. First, there is the essay on religion in Postmodernity and its Discontents *in which you seem to see religion as a remnant of the quest for ontological security; a remnant which is either irrelevant today or which takes the diseased form of 'fundamentalism'. Second, there is your book* Mortality, Immortality and Other Life Strategies *in which you grapple with questions which were long ago also confronted by the world religions (What is the meaning of death? What is the meaning of suffering?). And then, third, there is the increasing tendency of your writing to deploy biblical metaphors and imagery. A good example of this tendency is provided by your paper, 'What Prospects of Morality in Times of Uncertainty?'*

It would be interesting to know why Levinas pointed you in the direction of politics and not in the direction of theology and, in a word, God. Does Levinas point to an infinity beyond politics, yet also beyond sociological understanding?

ZYGMUNT BAUMAN   Our moral impulse, if we have one, has weak feet. It is not a good traveller and does not get more skilful and indefatigable as it grows older; it runs off its power faster than it moves. When embarking on a journey it gets weary quickly, and feels like resting and taking a nap as soon as it gets as far as the farm fence. At close distance, its eyes are sharp, but as the distance grows clear contours blur into a mist. And it is hard of hearing, cries for help coming from afar reach its ears with difficulty. It has delivered its message, a message we can hardly forget once we have heard it: acts are good or evil, and what they are depends on what benefit or harm they bring to other living creatures. But being a poor traveller, short-sighted and hard of hearing, it gets lost, lackadaisical and inept when away from home. Perhaps what we mean by 'home' is that small and cosy plot inside which our moral impulse, and the moral impulses of all the others inside, are alert and lively, eager to tell us where the line between good and evil lies and warn us against trespassing.

You know Hans Jonas's worry: armed with technological wonders, we can now carry the consequences of our actions far beyond the reaches of the family plot, indeed to awesome distances in space and time, to lands we will never bodily visit. As to the consequences of our actions, the powers of eyes and ears (or, for that matter, muscles) no longer set a limit. But our moral impulses have not followed suit. They still need eyes and ears, and their eyes and ears have not grown stronger (morality, says Jonas, is still in the state it was in at the time of Adam and Eve). I share Jonas's worry, though not his idea of what needs to be done to restore the lost balance. Jonas, as you know, put the buck on the philosophers' desks: put your heads together and think out the rules for a 'long-distance ethics'. I believe, though, that this is something we need least. We already know very well indeed what to do and what to desist from. We all know that wars and famines and pollution and humiliation are evils. But somehow, despite that knowledge, we all contribute to wars, famines, pollution and humiliation.

The real snag is that while knowing *what* to do (and what to avoid doing) we lack the agencies that could push human affairs the way we would wish them to go. It is not the *knowledge* of good and evil that we are missing; it is the skill and zeal to *act* on that knowledge which is conspicuously absent in this world of ours, in which dependencies, political responsibility and cultural values part ways and no longer hold each other in check. Between knowledge and action, between action and its consequences, gaps – frightful and potentially apocalyptic gaps – yawn.

It is in this sense that, in my reading, Levinas's decision to locate the issue of good and evil in human *condition* (rather than in human *artifices*, as Durkheim implied) leads to *politics*. As I have already mentioned on another occasion, politically operated justice is to moral capacity what transport technology is to the long-distance mobility of humans whose condition is to be upright and bipedal, but who are armed by nature only with a pair of legs. And I do not think that my reading is altogether idiosyncratic. When you go through the

brief pieces written, and the interviews given, by Levinas in
the last years of his life, you cannot but be struck by his
obsession with the fate of morality once it is exposed to the
cold winds blowing out there, outside the warm and cosy
shelter/incubator of the 'moral party of two'. Arne Johan
Vetlesen, who conducted one of these last interviews, told
me that during their conversation Levinas returned stubbornly to that issue whatever question he was asked.

What we miss, in other words, is not the sentiment and
not the knowledge, but the bridges capacious enough to
carry them back into human condition. And the gaps which
need to be spanned by those bridges are widening by the
day. Politics has never been needed as badly as it is now,
when it has fallen on hard times and lost much of its capacity
for bridge-building.

'Levinas's ethics points directly in the direction of theology'? I would agree with that, providing that we make clear
first what are we talking about. By the way, John Paul II
quoting Levinas signifies a movement of theology towards
ethics as much as it does the stretching of ethics towards
God. John Paul II is perhaps the greatest, the most whole-
some and outspoken *ethical philosopher* in the history of the
Papacy. His whole pontificate has been dedicated to the task
of restoring morality to its lost sovereignty over human-
being-in-the-world. The message he hammers home relentlessly, in every homily and with amazing consistency, is that
there is no excuse for surrendering or just suspending the
moral self's responsibility. Disempowering the moral self
was the prime sin of the Communist variety of totalitarianism, but the suggestion that moral dilemmas can be resolved,
or moral duties bypassed, with market-supplied gadgets
turns into the prime sin of the world that has emerged after
the fall of Communism. John Paul II does it all with
exquisite force, but what he has done is to resurrect the
'ethical bent' which was the most conspicuous mark of
Christianity, the creed whose birth-act was the deification
of self-sacrifice. In his scrupulous study of the relation
between Christian Agape and non-denominational Eros,

Anders Nygren pointed out that 'Agape may be compared to a stream flowing with immense force in a clearly defined channel', while 'Eros is a broad, shallow river with marshy banks.' Christianity has been a bold attempt to make Eros, that common yet stray and rambling human energy, into a tributary of the powerful river that irrigates the whole of humanity instead of nourishing just those few who happen to reside nearby.

Now back to the question of what we are talking about when we discuss the directions in which Levinas's ethics leads. Let me start with Levinas's God and His infinity. There is in French a semantic distinction between *l'autre* and *l'autrui* which is not always conveyed in the Levinas-inspired anglophone debates. If that distinction is respected, it will make sense to argue that 'the Other' stands in Levinas for alterity, and that it is alterity which is the ultimate mystery that Levinas insists on preserving (hallowing even) in its impenetrable and inalienable mysteriousness. God is such an absolute alterity (and so are, as Levinas avers in other contexts, the Future or the Woman). The absoluteness of alterity is at the same time a warning and a challenge. We cannot but stretch ourselves towards it. We wish to lock it in our embrace, but while reaching for it we must stay mindful of the ultimate hopelessness of that desire.

I sense in Levinas's narrative a primacy awarded to the tactile sense. The caress is the best metaphor for Levinas's idea of moral relationship, lovingly stroking the contours of the other's body while being wary of pressing it too hard, from making the grip too tight and uncomfortable for the caressed, and threatening to deform her or his shape. The self and alterity are bound to meet while staying in different universes. They are not commensurable, just as infinity cannot be fathomed, let alone exhausted, by anything as finite as the transient and mortal self. We cannot fulfil our desire, but neither can we stop trying to fulfil it. This is the breathtaking beauty and the heart-rending drama of the moral self's predicament. The Other, as long as she or he is approached as an exemplar of alterity, belongs to one family with God or the Future. She or he is unknowable, but being human we cannot stop wishing to know. Rather than saying that the Other leads Levinas (and through him, his followers) to God, I would say that the Other and God were in each other's company from the start and only by staying in that company do each of them 'make sense'.

I must confess to you that I never felt comfortable about the alleged boundary between the 'religious' and the 'secular', and most certainly never believed in the sanctity of that boundary. If you accept, as I do, Leszek Kolakowski's definition of religion as the admission of human insufficiency, then religion is something much more universal than any particular church, gospel or liturgy. One may say alternatively that this definition spells out religion's *genus proximum* yet neglects to name its *differentia specifica*. We, the humans, are flawed creatures, the finite beings thinking infinity, mortal beings sorely tempted by eternity, the unfinished beings dreaming of completion, the uncertain beings starved of certainty. We are, hopelessly, insufficient. For that reason either we are all irrevocably religious (if you name any feeling of insufficiency, in whatever verbal carapace it is inserted, 'religious'), or we are all hopelessly doomed to desperately seek an escape from that hopelessness, of which religion is one of the possible alternatives (if you agree with me that the feeling of insufficiency is religion's necessary, but not distinctive trait). Escape from insufficiency, a compensation for insufficiency, can be sought and pursued in more ways than sheltering in God's embrace.

The so-called 'secularization' of the modern era was not much more than the designation of a vocabulary which can be used to narrate the human predicament without using the word 'God'. The word could be missing, but the narrative, as before, has been all along about human insufficiency and the valiant struggle to cope with its potentially devastating consequences. There was no shortage of substitutes for the missing word (each signalling, if you wish, another reincarnation of God): Nature, Laws of History, Reason, Progress (man-made perhaps, but beyond the human power to arrest). Nietzsche wisely insinuated that God truly dies only when the Superman is born. But thus far, all the haughtiness of *techne* and all the arrogance of its PR representatives notwithstanding, the Superman has not been born, though most of us most of the time are offered tasks cut to his measure. Ulrich Beck's *Risikogesellschaft* is the latest rendering of the ancient insufficiency story. This time, though, it cannot be said to contain the promise of redemption.

Yes, indeed, I am turning, and ever more often, to biblical metaphors. The way the story of human experience, the human predicament of the finite beings thrown, always until-further-notice, in infinite time/space, has been recorded in the Bible has not been surpassed (or is it rather that having shaped our experience in the course of millennia, it has set the frame for all future recordings?). All other metaphors are pale by comparison. I frankly admit that as a story of the passage from nothingness to being I find the 'Big Bang' tale much poorer than the story of God's six-day job. And less illuminating. There is no character in that story to inform us, after the fractions of the first few seconds, whether what has emerged out of the pristine 'nothing' was good or bad. 'Big Bang' is a story of creation minus its edifying, moral message. It may flatter the conceit of human reason and replenish its occasionally flagging self-confidence (a do-it-yourself storytelling job may help us to forget that the narrated mystery is, at the end of the story, as humiliatingly mysterious as it was at the start), but it would hardly help the human carriers of reason to live more wisely.

If the ethicality of the human predicament stands in the focus of sociological inquiry, biblical stories have amply proved their unfading potency. The story of the origins of morality has been told in the Bible twice, each time differently. And since then all ethical philosophy has been but a regurgitation and recycling of those two stories. I find it exceedingly helpful to unwrap the substance of the dilemma (morality-through-uncertainty *versus* morality-through-obedience), which is otherwise difficult to glimpse beneath the thick and dense

crust of refined philosophical talk, by recalling the arche-
types recorded in the Bible.

I suspect that, all the audacity of the modern adventure
notwithstanding, the feeling of human insufficiency continues to grow, if anything, deeper, and that the existential
challenge to fill the gaps in the human capacity to cope is
nowhere near to being met. Modern hopes/ambitions/prom-
ises to compose a mystery-and-contingency-free territory for
human *Lebenswelt* fizzled out, and the efforts to keep them
alive have ground to a halt.

In *In Search of Politics* and in *Liquid Modernity* I tried to
comprehend why all that happened, and to figure out
whether one can think of ways to stop the process and
mitigate its consequences or alleviate the pain they cause.
Reviving the *agora*, that quintessentially political act, seems
to me to be the step from which all possible ways towards
that end would need to start.

I do not entertain hope that any of the ways that might
be chosen will put paid to human insufficiency. We seem to
be embroiled with it for richer and poorer, for better and
worse, and till death us do part. But between the poles of
human self-sufficiency and the drifting plankton-mode of
existence extends the vast area of human choice and action.
And both the choice and the action cannot but be political.

And it was Levinas who sent me on the road leading to
that conclusion.

*A key concept in Levinas's thought is totality. It refers to the
quest for power and control and to the organization of systems.
This meaning of totality resonates with your account and
depiction of the ordering designs of modernity. With Levinas
himself, the concept of totality leads to a view of the state as an
institution which is about totalization and which thereby
represses the infinity of the ethical demand. Totality is about
the Same, infinity is about the Other. However, throughout our
conversations you have stressed that the state in conditions of
'liquid modernity' is different from that typical of 'solid modernity'. The state is no longer in the business of totalization.*

Consequently, does your sociological appreciation of liquid modernity require a rethinking of Levinasian totality? To what extent are you trying to provide a sociological account of politics after totality?

Even the wisest among us can hardly step beyond the world which has formed us while being formed by our thoughts and deeds. Giants like Plato or Aristotle could not imagine a world without slavery, Bossuet would be baffled by a story of a world without monarchy. This seems to be a minor irritant though. We can all read Plato and Aristotle, and indeed Bossuet, to learn something vital about our world, and not just to pander to our curiosity for the long deceased past. Something truly to worry about is how not to overlook the changes in the world which call the bluff of the continuity implied by the inertia of our memory. Memory, I keep repeating, is a double-edged sword and all too often we swing that sword in the wrong direction.

Sniffing *today* the danger most awesome in Big Brother, panopticon or the totalitarian tendency endemic to the modern state is tantamount to misusing the sword of memory and causing self-inflicted wounds, instead of using that sword to cut a passage through the thicket of new and yet unexplored life realities (there is a popular expression for that kind of wrong focus of attention: barking up the wrong tree). Today, it is Pilate's gesture of hands-washing, rather than dirtying them in successive attempts to insert some logic into the messy human predicament, that constitutes the state's main contribution to human misery. Too much of the state is a catastrophe, but so is too little.

Invoking Beck once more: there are no biographical solutions to systemic contradictions, though this is precisely what the state washing its hands of its functions would like us to believe. I repeat: thrown at the big screen of society, the challenge of morality turns into the issue of justice, and fighting injustice can only be a collective affair, a matter for an autonomous, that is politically constituted, society. But as John Gray forcefully argues (in an essay written for a

comprehensive study of *Social Inclusion* collated by Peter
Askonas and Angus Stewart in 2000), 'the emergence of
social democratic governments across most of Europe has
done nothing to falsify' the supposition that the 'divisive
consequences of the workings of late capitalism in a context
of globalization' are unlikely to be reversed. Judging by their
performance to date, such governments are inclined to act
as 'the political vehicle for further neoliberal market reform',
that is, to put it in a nutshell, for the further withdrawal of
the state, the sole democratically controlled 'totality'
modernity has invented, from its responsibility for promoting social justice.

The worldwide 'informatic highway' has been widely
hailed as the harbinger of new, 'real' democracy of a kind
which the state with its easy-to-achieve control over knowledge would never have achieved nor wished to achieve. (The
worldwide spread of the new opportunity to 'participate' is,
of course, a lie; 88 per cent of the 'internauts' live in affluent
countries which accommodate but 17 per cent of world
population, while access to the internet among the working
classes of those countries, not to mention the impoverished
'underclass', is, and is likely to remain, negligible; the advent
of informatics has, if anything, further deepened the gap
between the developed and underdeveloped countries and
between the mighty and the indolent of any single society.)
It was also hailed as the ultimate liberation of 'civil society'
from the oppressive tutelage of the state and its bureaucracy.

Well, Durkheim famously suggested that emancipating
the individual from society, far from auguring individual
freedom, would usher into slavery. We may say that the
alleged liberation of 'civil society' from the state does not
serve the cause of freedom either. As Armand Mattelart
pointed out a few years ago (in *Le Monde de l'Éducation* of
April 1997), 'the techno-utopia' is an ideological weapon in
an ongoing 'traffic in influence' under the aegis of 'free
trade'. It is a part and parcel of the discourse in which the
state is represented as the evil enemy of the true freedom of
a politics-free 'civil society' of sovereign individuals. But, in

actual fact, the dismantling of (state) political constraints and controls, far from making 'civil society' free and truly autonomous, opens it to the unabashed rule of market forces which members of that society, now left to their own devices, have no means nor power to resist.

These days, the main obstacle to social justice is not the invasive intentions or proclivities of the state, but its growing impotence, aided and abetted daily by the officially adopted 'there is no alternative' creed. I suppose that the danger we will need to fight back in the coming century won't be totalitarian coercion, the main preoccupation of the century just ended, but the falling apart of 'totalities' capable of securing the autonomy of human society.

Indeed, the network of dependencies which determine the condition under which we live and frame our choices has become global, but the globalization of dependencies has not been followed by a globalization of democratic control and its controlling/guiding/correcting abilities. Just as our moral impulses froze at the level available to Adam and Eve in their small and cosy world, a level insufficient to grapple with the big issues of social justice, so our justice-promoting instruments froze at the level of the nation-state, an institution sorely inadequate to cope with the production of injustice located far beyond its reach, in the global space. Concerns and stratagems born of yesterday's fears and designed to fight yesterday's dangers are singularly unfit to resist the dangers of today and placate today's fears.

Wise after the fact, we are painfully aware now of the dangers of 'totality' once it is given a free rein and allowed to run amuck. But so we should also be aware of the threats that are hiding in the kind of world in which the 'totalities' able to control and contain it are no longer generated, let alone kept in a working order.

So yes, Levinasian 'totality' needs rethinking. I would suppose that Levinas would be the first to engage in such rethinking were he around to note how much the sets of the political scene have been refurbished and reshuffled. But it is not only the Levinasian sort of 'totality' that needs rethinking. The classic 'critical theory' operated within the same cognitive horizons as Levinas and also needs intense rethinking.

In a number of essays and books you have written acidly about communitarian politics, and this coincides with what amounts to a more widespread suspicion of contemporary communities which can be found in your work (a suspicion which is represented in your small book on Community*). Is your suspicion towards community – and by extension communitarianism – a representation of your ethical critique of totality?*

I am indeed suspicious of the medicine peddled by the *communitarians*. As for *community*, the matter is not that straightforward. As I tried to argue in the little book you've mentioned, we cannot help missing the missing community, but the community we miss cannot stop being missing. Most certainly, it cannot be commissioned, 'made on demand' and 'to order', and the efforts to deny and defy that impossibility cause a lot of human misery of their own. There is a lot of sabre-rattling going on in the world in the name of would-be communities and loyalty to their cause, and lucky are the people in whose neighbourhood the hubbub stops at the rattling of sabres.

Communities with a hope for a long (though not necessarily happy) life need a baptism of fire; complicity to the 'original crime' is the best warrant for a longish life expectation. The awesome truth is that far from being an outburst of insufficiently tamed or inadequately socialized passions which modern reason had no time to exterminate, the explosive origins of newly projected communities are more often than not the outcomes of sober rationality, very much in line with impeccably modern 'rational choice' precepts. Neglecting that connection while waxing lyrical about the beauties of community life and the bliss that will follow its refoundation means – literally – playing with fire. There are reasons to be suspicious whenever the call 'let us now praise the community' is heard.

This is why I am wary of the communitarian cure for the present trouble, just as I'd be wary of falling from the frying-pan into the fire. Besides, even leaving aside the gory side-effects of community foundation and pugnacious defence, we would be well advised to remember what the ostensibly warm and comfortable embrace of community once stood accused of during those now distant times when it was still experienced daily. Communal life is unlikely to be experienced as an unmitigated bliss. The right to fight back the conformizing pressures and to escape the dreary, grinding monotony of sameness has been a hard-won achievement which few of us would be happy to forfeit. True, the community dreams are natural and fully understandable in people rehearsing daily the unprepossessing loneliness of 'disembedded individuals'; but this does not necessarily mean that they would find the fulfilment of their dreams any more appetizing. The fulfilment of dreams may only usher into horrors different from the ones suffered thus far.

The present-day born-again communitarianism is an understandable reaction to the ever-more-obvious impotence of the state which was once looked to hopefully or feared for its assumed omnipotence. The promises now dropped by the state these days lie on the ground waiting to be picked up by agents deemed more reliable because of not having yet been tried and discredited. Security, certainty, collective insurance against individually suffered misfortune; all seem now to be waiting for DIY handling; for the 'community' of 'people like us' and most resolutely 'unlike them' ready to take matters into their own hands.

It is this vision of 'people like us' and 'unlike them' (complete with the purification rites and intolerance to difference which inevitably follow), ubiquitously present in any communitarian dream and virtually impossible to pare off without the whole thing simply falling apart, that I find particularly worrying. Humanity, as Jean-Pierre Marniere nicely put it, is 'a machine to produce differences', and it took centuries to recognize this truth and to accept it as an inalienable ingredient of the human lot. It would be sad if we were in one fell swoop to forfeit that difficult, yet precious, gain hoping (wrongly) that the difficulty of being human will go away. Our variety and our differences make us all richer in our humanity, that condition which will never be easy to bear but which we can make more (or less!) fascinating, challenging, creative and enjoyable.

The idea of 'human rights' means, first and foremost, the right to be different and to have this difference respected. Difference is one aspect of humanity which cannot be 'nationalized', 'communalized' and otherwise expropriated from the human individuals to whom it belongs without delivering a mortal blow to the very idea of human rights, the right to the dignity of being human. And yet while the attempts to nationalize the difference fade and lose much of their clout, expropriation as such has not ground to a halt. 'Communalization' has come to offer the services which the state, as the nation's plenipotentiary, abandoned, or lost interest in (and need for).

I agree with another Bauman (Gerd, with a double 'n'), when he castigates Charles Taylor, and through him other advocates of currently fashionable 'multiculturalism' (in *The Multicultural Riddle*), for tacitly assuming a reified nature of culture(s), for thinking of cultures as like 'things' complete inside and clearly delineated on the outside (one may say: a coconut and an avocado rolled into one), and overlapping with 'societies', understood as populations in their terri-tories. 'If multiculturalism is indeed a "politics of recog-nition", as Taylor says, what then is it that is to be recognized?' asks Baumann, and I after him. 'Is it one of those reified "cultures", perhaps that of a local majority whose leaders are most adept at essentializing its norms for survival? Or should we recognize cultural diversity, that is the commitment of citizens and residents to recognize the dialogical nature of all their identities?' Culture, here again I see eye to eye with Gerd, 'is not an imposition of fixed and normed identities, but a dialogical process of making sense with and through others.'

What we are talking about here is the republican model,

the kind of togetherness which is founded in the commitment to continuous dialogue, and assigning to that dialogue
the prerogatives of the supreme court in which values are
examined and assessed, and in which binding verdicts are
passed and appeals against the verdicts are lodged. It is only
in such a republican setting that communities may be
formed, entered and exited as the human rights sustained by
the republic allow and require.

In books like Postmodern Ethics *and* Life in Fragments *you
talk about a 'politics of distant consequences'. Could you outline
what that phrase means and what you take such a politics to
involve?*

We have briefly discussed this issue before. I gather that it
boils down to the incipient, but fast growing imbalance
between the means that we (as members of humankind)
have at our disposal and deploy, and the ends which we
(individually, severally, collectively, all together) see as worthy of our attention and effort. That imbalance is exactly
the opposite to what Max Weber anticipated when sketch-
ing the future of modern capitalism as a kingdom of *instrumental* rationality: ends are given, let us find (invent or
discover) the best means. Ours are, on the contrary, the
times of answers seeking questions, solutions seeking problems, means seeking applications. The objectives of action
(those thought of and deliberately chosen, and those
unthought of and emerging as a surprise) are the major
sources of risk and uncertainty. All too often we learn of
their nature after the fact; we call them then 'unanticipated
consequences'. That most actions have unwholesome and
unpleasant consequences ('side-effects', 'collateral damage',
etc.) which we would try to avoid were they known to us in
advance is by now a trivial observation. But somehow that
awareness does not stop risky steps from being taken, short-
term and localized actions being undertaken and seen
through. It seems to us to be a shame and a sin, and above
all an unforgivable waste, not to use the means which are

already available. We will worry about the consequences when they fall upon us, hoping that it will be other people who will need to worry.

But please note: more often than not the 'unanticipated' nature of certain off-putting consequences is not a matter of insufficient or erroneous *knowledge*, but of political decision-making. The difference between 'product' and 'waste', between the 'effect' and the 'side-effect', is 'objective' in no other sense than that of the superior strength of those who draw the lines by comparison to those who fall on the receiving side. These divisions are contentious and contested, and this contest is the stuff of politics. Deciding what is what, setting apart the 'legitimate' ends of action from its perhaps unpleasant, but 'secondary' and 'unavoidable' side-effects, are matters (stakes) of power struggles. The hope of rendering the 'unavoidable' avoidable, or to anticipate the 'unanticipated', should be invested in the progress of politics, and not (certainly not *only*) in the progress of science and technology.

As the means grow unstoppably and at an accelerating pace, so do the consequences of their application. But the means do not *just* grow; they tend to polarize. Their distribution within humankind is highly uneven, and imbalances in the distribution grow arguably faster still than the total volume of means. With the growth of means and of the inequality of their allocation, the power to separate the desirable (or tolerable) from the 'unanticipated' (or unbearable) tends to be polarized as well. This situation will continue as long as certain effects of action can be, with no penalty or at a tolerable cost, left out of calculation. And leaving them out of calculation, dismissing them as 'collateral damage' or as a side-and-minor effect will remain a possibility, a tempting and eagerly jumped at possibility, as long as the reactions of those affected and suffering from the result may be neglected, prevented from being voiced, or if voiced then easily silenced or better still made inaudible. Again, we are back in the field of politics. 'Morality at a distance' can only take a political form, and the politics of

justice is a moral postulate; indeed, it is a moral response to
the appearance of The Third, to living in society, being a
society.

If it is to be effective, this politics, like any other effective
politics, requires laws. Let us not confuse, however, law and
totalitarianism. The opposite of totalitarianism is not law-
lessness (though the totalitarian ideologists would wish us to
believe this), but a system of law which guards human
rights; something like an extended and generalized version
of the old principle 'no taxation without representation'.

The other problem arising from the lengthening of the
'causation chain', from the far-reaching effects of actions, is,
in moral terms (though thus far not in legal or political
terms), the *globalization of responsibility*. At no time before
has John Donne's famous dictum ('No man is an island . . .
every man is a piece of the Continent'; 'Any man's death
diminishes me, because I am involved in Mankind. And
therefore never send to know for whom the bell tolls; it tolls
for thee') carried so much flesh; no longer is it but a poetic
invocation of noble yet lofty compassion. It is now a factual
report of genuine, tangible links which connect the plight of
as all. We all bear responsibility for whatever happens to
any of us, and the postulate of taking responsibility for our
responsibility now involves the need to alleviate sufferings
in whatever spot of the globe they may happen, the most
distant sufferings included. This new challenge stretches the
endurability of the 'moral impulse' to its limit (perhaps
beyond its limit), considering that for long centuries that
impulse used to operate (and so has learned to feel truly at
home) only in the proximity of the Other. Now it needs to
embrace a distant, actually an 'abstract' Other, an 'Other'
unlikely ever to be met, and a misery hardly ever to be
confronted point-blank.

Intrepid and indefatigable TV crews from time to time
bring the pictures of that distant misery into our homes.
This has an instant effect, as all proximity to human suffering tends to have. It cuts the enormity of new responsibilities
to the capacity of our moral sensitivity. Is that, though,

enough to measure up to the magnitude of the challenges? The common result of mass media campaigns is, as you yourself have pointed out in your studies, a succession of 'carnivals of pity' and periods of 'charity fatigue'. There are, periodically, outbursts of compassion, but there is but so much and no more that our moral sentiments can carry on their own; soon placated, they take a nap until the next 'event' when they are once more brutally awakened to the fact that nothing much has changed in the volume and depth of human misery despite the short-lived explosions of pity.

By their nature, media-led 'carnivals of pity' are ill-equipped to sediment a solidly institutionalized, permanent and effective link out of the momentary flashes of the 'we are all pieces of the same continent' feelings. They bring home the horrifying likeness of human suffering, but stop far short of laying bare its causes such as the livelihoods destroyed by free trade, soil devastated by market-imposed monocultures, or the tribal enmities aided and abetted by the arms industry and the traffic that fills the coffers of our treasury and beefs up our domestic GNP. No wonder that the roots of misery remain intact, however successful the successive 'humanitarian aid' campaigns might have been. Besides, our own, direct or indirect, responsibility for the misery we so sincerely pity remains undisclosed. It seems as if we did not owe anything to those miserable people; whatever we do for them should not be seen as an attempt to repay our debts and repent our sins but be praised as the expression of our noble sentiments, thus adding to our moral glory.

The multifarious complexities of 'distant suffering', and the challenges they posit to us as ethical and political beings, have been exhaustively indexed and scrutinized by Luc Boltanski in his *La Souffrance à distance*. Boltanski put under the microscope the emergent 'humanitarian movements' (more often than not successions of intermittent campaigns rather than movements, to be sure) and wondered how, if at all, the scattered, haphazard and all-too-often short-lived responses to the sight of distant misery could be consolidated into a permanent net of institutions, strong enough to countervail and possibly arrest the ongoing immiseration of vast chunks of the globe which we share, and of large groups of our fellow humans. Such a consolidation of a humanitarian movement, Boltanski suggests, 'depends, at least in part, on its ability to clarify and make explicit the connection, which is often realized in practice by its members, between distant causes and the traditions, sensibilities and even interests of those who organize support for these causes'. Even when (and if) such a connection is revealed and brought home, a systematic and regular (as distinct from an emotional and ephemeral) response is, however, far from certain to follow. This is for a number of reasons, among which the widespread 'scepticism with regard to any form of political action orientated towards a horizon of moral ideals' and the 'loss of confidence in the effectiveness of committed speech' loom particularly large. The same quandary again: politics on the scale of extended (global) dependencies, political agency on a par with the grandiosity of the task.

We have a long way to go to arrive there, but we can slow down only at our – joint and shared – peril.

We have been moving around the problem of totality and infinity, of ethical distance and moral proximity. In your work – and indeed in these conversations – the problem has often taken the form of a concern with the dominance of the market leading to transient attachments to places and peoples, to the concern with the self leading to fleeting relationships with others and with the rise of a widespread privatization of individuality and everyday life. Meanwhile, globalization continues to wreck local economies and environments and it continues to lead to a world which no individual can control or even understand, except through the risks and anxieties that it promotes. And nation-states cannot assuage those risks and anxieties because, as we all know thanks to the tenets of the so-called third way, this is a world in which insecurity is inevitable and must be confronted.

The discussion of the fate of the classical agora *which runs through* In Search of Politics *can be seen in this context; you talk about the* agora *because that is the classical space and place of politics which seems to be challenged by all of the processes and relationships of liquid modernity. The* agora *is a place and a space of a politics of proximity, company and the face-to-face in a way which makes it rest easily with a Levinas-inspired ethics. But can these concepts which are derived from classical political theory and time-honoured models of democracy possess any relevance in the contemporary situation, where the face-to-face has been desensitized and made one-way by television and in which public spaces seem to occasion feelings of fear and danger rather more than any engagements of sociation and company?*

Nothing to add, nothing to detract from your description of the fragmentation and episodicity of social bonds and human attachments.

On one occasion I met a brilliant (still young, but just) researcher who had worked for various BBC programmes for around fourteen years. He was good in the jobs he did, so he kept being gladly employed by the producers of successive broadcasts. But when we met he had not earned anything like 'tenure' as yet. He lived from one project to another, having little idea what his chances would be when the current project was completed. He did not like that life very much, but he expected this 'job situation' to last. I suspect that by the time we met he was coming to accept it as 'normal'. Boltanski and Chiapello suggest that the fate of that BBC researcher is a pattern for things to come, for the way in which we all will be 'riveted' (very loosely, it looks) into society. Permanent buildings cannot be erected on quicksand, and it would be utterly foolish to try (as well as dangerous for the daredevils who do it). Employers are reluctant to commit themselves for the long term, and they've stopped expecting long-term commitments from their employees. They want from them total, twenty-four-hours-a-day dedication to a job at hand, but no 'loyalty for life', no identification with the company, which would only cramp their own freedom to move and change. Jobs that need to be performed may change tomorrow, and no one can tell what form they will take, what sort of action will be required and what sort of experience and know-how will become redundant. What the employers favour in the people they wish to hire is versatility, flexibility and adaptability, facility in accepting a changed scenario and in quitting without murmur once there are no more lines left for the character in which they had been cast (indeed, the ability and the will to 'finish quickly and to begin from the beginning', in Pascal's phrase).

Giddens's 'pure relationships', entered fast and dissolved on demand, tend to mark this struggle for livelihood as much as they do the intimate partnerships people weave while making sure that they may be abandoned once they no longer bring pleasure. Here and there life runs from one 'project' to another, each of them 'for the time being', none of them presumed to last indefinitely. The main point an employee has to prove when employed in a current project is his or her employability in future, similarly fixed-term, projects. And this can be accomplished not by showing oneself to be a 'natural' for the job currently performed, but to be fit for many jobs, as many as they come and as varied as they are and yet may be.

And so we are all, not necessarily by choice, bound over and over again to 'finish quickly and start again from the beginning', and we are in for a lot of frustration and despair if we expect others around us not to follow the same precept. 'Long-term commitment' is turning into a liability. It is instead freedom from commitments that becomes an asset. Life looks increasingly like a series of new starts, and becomes a continuous experimentation with new options, untested styles and unexplored opportunities.

The 'rational choice' theorists are quick to point out that the pattern spreads to political behaviour as well. More and

more, electors behave like consumers of fleeting opportunities. Loyalty 'for better or worse, come what may' no
longer guides their choices. In politics, as in all the rest of
the 'lived world', focuses of attention and the idols or
celebrities that occupy them rise and disappear with great
and growing speed. This circumstance cannot but spell
trouble for the *agora*. The 'we will meet again' feeling, the
expectation that whatever is being done will have lasting
consequences which all who do it will suffer or witness, the
belief that all sides are bound by their acts and will stay
around long enough to be held to account in case they fail
to do their duty (indeed, the trust grounded in the conviction that however hurly-burly the political game may seem
on the surface, it is *not* a random collection of 'new beginnings', unbound by the past and not binding the future), are
what makes time in the *agora* well spent, and the debates
conducted in the *agora* a sensible pastime. When the credi-
bility of such beliefs keeps being sapped and refuted by daily
experience, a 'rational voter' would no longer bother with
the humdrum, prosaic and tedious business of politics. The
agora is refurbished and redeployed as a theatre, where new
spectacles (happenings, rather) are staged with few actors,
but with crowds of spectators attracted by the promise of
fun and expected to do no more than get their share of
excitement, applaud or whistle.

The business of tying together proximity and distance and
keeping them in a continuous dialogue, the job which the
agora was expected to be good at, is ever more difficult, and
perhaps impossible, to perform.

Who, in liquid modernity, are the agents of politics?

Yes, the crisis of agency is the centre point of the trouble
democratic politics is presently going through. John Major's
series of 'citizen's charters' grasped the trend very well
indeed, though by default rather than by design. With
amazing consistency, it stripped the 'citizen' of all her or his
duties except that of clamouring for better services. It

redefined the citizen as the consumer of goods supplied by the ministerial companies. It found no other role for the citizen. In particular, it had nothing to say about the contribution the citizen can make to the laws of the country, about the say he might have in their formation – let alone his right to be present, heard and listened to when the agenda of law-making is under consideration.

It would be idle – and unjust – to blame the politicians alone for this ongoing expropriation of the citizen. They may be blamed for not telling the truth, the whole truth and nothing but the truth about the power shifts which happen in the world we jointly inhabit, and thus rendering a sensible resistance to the shifts more difficult yet than it has already been. They may be blamed, above all, for the 'there is no alternative' excuse (a fraudulent one, to be sure) to which they resort so keenly whenever another surrender, and so another step to the disempowerment of citizenry, is on the cards. But it is hardly the shape of the world that their half-truths and lies gloss over.

As to that shape, two parallel and closely connected processes make it what it is. First is seemingly unstoppable globalization, which takes power out of politics, and economics (the reproduction of livelihood) out of political control. Second is a complex process awkwardly dubbed 'individualization', consisting in the 'phasing out', one by one, of all societally woven and serviced safety nets at the time when individuals are called on to jump, each one on her or his own and to be bold and daring when they do. The first process strips interest and involvement in politics of much of its practical sense and so of attraction. The second makes it unlikely that the interest in politics would be expressed in any way that counts.

Powers flow away, unimpeded, from politics. As Rorty pithily put it, 'globalization is producing a world economy in which an attempt by any one country to prevent the immiseration of its workers may result only in depriving them of employment. This world economy will soon be owned by a cosmopolitan upper class which has no more sense of community with any workers anywhere than the great American capitalists of the year 1900 had with the immigrants who manned their enterprise.' However brave the faces which the professional politicians make, and however juicy the plums they may promise their electors in exchange for their once-in-five-years loyalty, this is the sorry truth of contemporary politics. Governments can do little to mitigate the gnawing pain of uncertainty; to cut at its roots they can do nothing. They are, after all, sorely local, and power nowadays is exterritorial and could not, and need not, care about pugnacious voices or dashing gestures made in any locality. If voices and gestures are indeed made, the punishment will be swift and conclusive. But the sheer threat of punishment would prove in most cases (most politicians are, after all, rationally thinking beings) to be a sufficient deterrent.

As to the second process, passing under the enticing but misleading name of 'individualization', having been exposed, one at a time, to the blows of fortune striking at random and picking its victims by mysterious, unfathomable standards only loosely if at all related to what the prospective victims or those who are (temporarily) saved might have done, no wonder the individuals-by-decree-of-fate fail to see how they could blend together their individually suffered troubles and then recast them as a common cause. Even less can they see how their chances of survival, let alone of getting on top of things, could gain from joining forces and so justify the sacrifice which a cause proclaimed to be common would require.

Each of the two processes adds force to the other and supplies credible arguments for its unstoppability. Together, they sow and fertilize the seeds of the 'no-alternative' creed.

The question today is not to ask who are the agents of politics, but who are the agents capable of remarrying now divorced power and politics, and capable of restoring politics as a joint matter of 'the council and the people', the only form in which politics may provide the two-way link between an autonomous society and its autonomous citi-

zens. Both the 'council' and the 'people' have yet to be
created, though. We do not have a council; and to have one,
we need to raise ourselves to the status of the 'global
people'.

It is often said that the contemporary political situation is one
in which we must learn to live and think between the old
polarities of right and left, to embrace some centre course. Would
you accept that the purportedly old divisions between right and
left are no longer applicable? It is quite clear that you remain a
socialist at heart, and yet, if we are to believe all that we are
told to believe, socialism is a vestige of a time gone by.

I am glad you find me a socialist. I am indeed socialist (or so
at least I hope). I suppose that this world of ours needs
socialists more than at any other time, and that this need
has become much more poignant and urgent yet after the
fall of the Berlin Wall. It was capitalism's perverse luck that
Communism, more in its capacity as a spectre and an
apparition, a promise and a temptation, than in any of its
practical avatars, breathed behind its back through most of
its history. It was this spectre that provided the 'checking-
and-balancing' contraption which capitalism needed as badly
as it resented it. No alternative 'check-and-balance' mechanism is currently in operation; nor is one in sight. In its
absence, capitalism is marching joyfully and triumphantly
towards an abyss (Schumpeter prophesied that it will arrive
there thanks to its success), beckoning to us, like Captain
Ahab to his fellow sailors when strapped to Moby Dick's
back, to follow suit.

Our conversations have pondered the indignity of humiliation. Nothing humiliates more than poverty, and no poverty humiliates more than poverty suffered amidst people
bent on fast and accelerating enrichment. To imagine that
other forms of humiliation (and there is no shortage of
them) can equal the sufferings which are endemic to the
prospectless life amidst an orgy of ever more seductive
opportunities, the life of miserly handouts amidst the revelry

of fabulous made-overnight fortunes and golden handshakes, the sight of children waking up hungry and going to bed famished amidst the opulence spilling out from every shop-window, means to grasp a chance of a temporary respite from guilty conscience at the expense of a lie. And it is an illusion which only the well-off can entertain so long as the supply of booze does not run out and the time of sobering-up does not arrive. Poverty is not one humiliation among many socially caused humiliations – and not just because of being the most painful and causing more suffering to its victims than the victims of other kinds of humiliation may live through. It is a 'meta-humiliation' of sorts, a soil on which all-round indignity thrives, a trampoline from which 'multiple humiliation' is launched.

And the unbridled market forces, precisely for being unbridled, cannot but spawn a lot of poverty and ever growing numbers of the impoverished. Once let off the leash, they also push the impoverished deeper into the precipice of indignity, as the rest who have been spared the lot of the poor climb to ever new heights of affluence.

Socialism, to me at least, is not an alternative model of society bound to replace the currently operating system. Socialism is a sharp knife pressed against the blatant injus-tices of society as it is, a voice of conscience bent on spoiling the self-conceit and self-adoration of John Kenneth Gal-braith's 'contented majority'. Consequently, it is a challenge to the society as it is never to stop questioning its wisdom, to think again about alternatives to its present state (a but-one-of-the-many-possible states) and of the ways of self-correction.

Socialism, to me at least, is not aimed against any model of society on condition that this society puts to the test its ability to correct the injustices and redeem the sufferings it has itself brought about. Socialism is aimed instead against the Panglosses of this world, both in the condensed and radicalized renditions of a Fukuyama who, having announced the end of historical choices, proclaims the out-come of the last choice to be the best of the possible worlds humanity is able to conceive, and in the diluted (yet not much less poisonous) form of the advocates of the 'for good or bad, there is no alternative' creed. Denying socialism that edge means rubbing salt into the open and festering wounds of poverty, that 'mother of all humiliation'.

Is socialism 'a vestige of a time gone by'? Were it indeed the case, we should be grateful to the 'time gone by' for leaving us such a vestige, no less than we are grateful to it for the rest of our civilized heritage. But it is not the case. Like the phoenix, socialism is reborn from every pile of ashes left day in, day out, by burned-out human dreams and charred hopes. It will keep on being resurrected as long as the dreams are burnt and the hopes are charred, as long as human life remains short of the dignity it deserves and the nobility it would be able, given a chance, to muster. And if it were the case, I hope I'd die a socialist.

Well, I owe you another confession. In terms of assumed political/ideational divisions, I happen to be a liberal in addition to being a socialist. Being both and not wishing to surrender either of the two souls is a recipe for a life full of doubts and difficult, never unambiguously good, choices. I believe, though, that socialist and liberal programmes, unless ossified into dogmas and transformed into windowless fortresses through years of trench war, are complementary rather than inimical. Security of livelihood, that *conditio sine qua non* of the human right to dare to fulfil one's potential, and freedom, that ability to act on that right, are two values which cannot be traded off completely without putting paid to human dignity (though they are constantly traded off, thereby making human dignity an ideal rather than the accomplished reality, a goal ever yet-to-be-attained; human dignity is bound to remain forever *in statu nascendi*).

It cannot be a matter of aberration, flawed logic or personal inconsistency that the greatest liberals arrived as a rule at socialist ideas while relentlessly following the inner logic of freedom as the supreme value of human life. That was the case of John Stuart Mill, and it seems to be the case of that most consistent of living liberals, Richard Rorty, when, in *Achieving Our Country*, he picks the deteriorating wages and the rampant disempowerment of the deprived, cast-out and downtrodden as the major obstacles to freedom, when he calls on the American Left to 'talk much more about money', castigates it for its 'retreat from activism' and 'disengagement from practice' and caustically observes that to many contemporary leftists 'stories about hegemony and power' are what the 'stories about blue-eyed devils are to the Black Muslims'. Rorty moves as far as demanding, following in the footsteps of Whitman or Dewey, the substitution of 'social justice for individual freedom as our country's principal goal'. This, to be sure, means going an inch or two beyond the line I myself would be prepared to cross. I am painfully aware that to strike the flawless, 'perfect' balance between justice and freedom is like squaring the circle. But I believe as well that the only chance that both justice and freedom have lies in our never-ending effort to balance them while avoiding all 'substitutes' and reducing to a minimum the pains which any trade-off must bring in its wake.

To the question of human dignity there are no simple solutions. But the most awesome of all threats to human dignity is to assume that the solutions are simple.

In the first conversation, you said that you have never entirely lost faith in the claim that sociology can change the world, although, you said, 'I have changed radically my view of the way in which the job of changing could, and should, be performed.' From what view did you change and to what view did you move? But some people might object that nowadays sociology cannot change anything except the self-understanding of men and women, while leaving the processes of globalization to cause the worlds of economics and war to separate more and more from what men and women can actually do anything about . . .

'Sociology cannot change anything except the self-understanding'?! What is this 'except' supposed to mean? Is not 'changing self-understanding' already a titanic task?! If only we could be sure that we are up to that task. We are, after all, but one of the many voices vying to capture human attention, by no means a particularly strong voice, not strong enough to be clearly audible in the cacophony of sounds, and most conspicuously not strong enough to stifle the silent pressures of the daily bustle which all too often make quite opposite messages credible.

Yes, on the door through which I once believed social reflection to be able and destined to enter social reality I would rather hang today the 'entry prohibited' sign, regretting that it has not been done before. That was the door of legislation within which right choices ought to be unambiguously determined by the carefully designed setting in which they are made, and the errors endemic to free choice and free experimentation excluded in advance. I do not believe that people may be forced into freedom (at the beginning of the last century such a belief was an error of judgement; at the beginning of the present century it is a crime). Prisons are known never to teach the art of free life. I no longer believe (as I did, to my shame, once believe) that 'the ends justify the means', and I do not believe it for the simple reason that ends cannot be humane if they require inhuman means to be promoted. And so the dialogue with the experience of free men and women is the only door which can be used. That does not by itself mean that it *will* be used; a lot of effort is needed to open it and keep it open.

Interpretative dialogue is a never-ending task and all along an uphill struggle. What it is not is an *alternative* to, or a substitute for, the focusing on the task of stopping the blind forces (of globalization, social polarization, exclusion, tribalism, etc.) in their tracks and warding off their morbid impact on the human condition. Far from standing in opposition to that task, the dialogic renegotiation of human experience is the *conditio sine qua non* of any chance of its fulfilment. One task requires the other, lest the effort to fulfil it stays ineffective.

In Luc Boltanski's formulation, the way to end or at least

mitigate human suffering leads through 'joining together', 'a description of the person suffering and the concern of someone informed of the suffering'. And this is precisely what the 'change of understanding' amounts to! Boltanski points out as well that 'one can commit oneself through speech' (and, let me add, one prompts others to commit themselves through dialogue) and points out, rightly, that one of the causes of the difficulty in overcoming the present crisis of understanding is 'a loss of confidence in the effectiveness of committed speech'. We can hardly arouse confidence in our partners-in-dialogue unless we go about earnestly proving that the confidence is not unfounded.

And so: was Weber right? Ought politics and science to be vocations?

The question is not whether they *ought* to be. It is rather *how to make them* be. And this is unlikely to be a one-off feat. Vocations, unlike other pastimes, tend to be lifelong.

Notes

The epigraph to the book is from Italo Calvino, *Invisible Cities*, trans. William Weaver, London: Secker and Warburg, 1974.

Conversation 1: Context and Sociological Horizons

1   The Polish October is the name given to the events which broke out in Poland in 1956 after Khrushchev's denunciation of Stalinism to the Twentieth Congress of the Communist Party of the Soviet Union. In Poland, the Communist Party used the moment to try to wrest power from the military and in June 1956 blood was spilt during riots in Poznan. Gomulka was appointed as head of the Polish Communist Party and resisted pressure to get matters back under the kind of control that Moscow desired. Gomulka's defiance of the Soviet Union reached a head in October 1956 when he stood firm against the threat of Soviet military intervention. Gomulka set Poland along its own path of socialism but, after October, he made sure that a firm cap was put on any criticisms of the Soviet Union. According to the historian Norman Davies, a 'deal was struck – an autonomous, national brand of Communism in return for continuing subservience to the USSR. The Polish People's Republic ceased to be a puppet state, and became a client state' (*Heart of Europe: A Short History of Poland*, Oxford University Press, 1986, pp. 10–11). As such, the Polish October is seen as a sign of dashed hopes and of an aborted freedom for Poland. Leszek Kolakowski puts it this way: 'The "Polish October", as it was called, far from ushering in a period

of social and cultural renewal or "liberalization", stood for the gradual extinction of all such attempts' (1978: 454).

2   *The Editor* is a news digest magazine published every Friday with the *Guardian* newspaper. Every week there is an item called 'The digested read' in which a new book in the headlines is subjected to a short review of a couple of hundred words under the title: 'Too busy to read the hot books? Let us read them for you.' The book is also reviewed in about twenty words under the banner: 'And if you are really pressed: the digested read, digested.'

Conversation 3: The Ambivalence of Modernity

1   The reference to 'Dover-style anti-immigration riots' is an allusion to the disturbances in the port of Dover during spring 2000, motivated by a 'moral panic' about the supposed influx of Roma and East European 'economic refugees' into England.

Bibliography

The first part of this bibliography gives details of texts written by Zygmunt Bauman and which are mentioned in the conversations and in the introduction. It is not at all a comprehensive list of Bauman's books. The second part of this bibliography gives details of texts which are specifically referred to in the course of the conversations and in the introduction. On a number of occasions Zygmunt Bauman refers in passing to an author, and in those cases the bibliography gives an example of a book (or in a few cases a couple of books) by that author which can be taken to be indicative of the kind of work which Bauman has in mind when he mentions them. As such, these references should be treated as points of departure for further reading and thinking.

Works by Zygmunt Bauman

(1969) 'Modern Times, Modern Marxism', in Peter L. Berger (ed.), *Marxism and Sociology: Views from Eastern Europe*, New York: Appleton Century Crofts.

(1972) 'Culture, Values and Science of Society', *University of Leeds Review*, vol. 15, pp. 185–203.

(1973) *Culture as Praxis*, London: Routledge and Kegan Paul.

(1976) *Socialism: The Active Utopia*, London: George Allen and Unwin.

(1978) *Hermeneutics and Social Science: Approaches to Understanding*, London: Hutchinson.

(1987) *Legislators and Interpreters: On Modernity, Post-modernity and Intellectuals*, Cambridge: Polity.

(1988) *Freedom*, Milton Keynes: Open University Press.

(1989) *Modernity and the Holocaust*, Cambridge: Polity.

(1991) *Modernity and Ambivalence*, Cambridge: Polity.

(1992a) *Intimations of Postmodernity*, London: Routledge.

(1992b) *Mortality, Immortality and Other Life Strategies*, Cambridge: Polity.

(1993) *Postmodern Ethics*, Cambridge: Polity.

(1995) *Life in Fragments: Essays in Postmodern Morality*, Cambridge: Polity.

(1997) *Postmodernity and its Discontents*, Cambridge: Polity.

(1998a) *Globalization: The Human Consequences*, Cambridge: Polity.

(1998b) *Work, Consumerism and the New Poor*, Buckingham: Open University Press.

(1998c) 'What Prospects of Morality in Times of Uncertainty?', *Theory, Culture and Society*, vol. 15(1), pp. 11–22

(1999a) *Culture as Praxis*, 2nd edn, London: Sage.

(1999b) *In Search of Politics*, Cambridge: Polity.

(1999c) 'The World Inhospitable to Levinas', *Philosophy Today*, vol. 43(2); extended version in Bauman 2000b: 'Private Morality, Immoral World', pp. 175–200.

(2000a) *Liquid Modernity*, Cambridge: Polity.

(2000b) *The Individualized Society*, Cambridge: Polity.

(2001) *Community*, Cambridge: Polity.

Works by others

Anderson, Benedict (1983) *Imagined Communities: Reflections on the Origin and Spread of Nationalism*, London: Verso.

Arendt, Hannah (1962) *The Origins of Totalitarianism*, London: George Allen and Unwin.

Arendt, Hannah (1977) *Eichmann in Jerusalem: A Report on the Banality of Evil*, Harmondsworth: Penguin.

Askonas, Peter and Stewart, Angus (eds) (2000) *Social Inclusion: Possibilities and Tensions*, London: Macmillan.

Bauman, Janina (1986) *Winter in the Morning: A Young Girl's Life in the Warsaw Ghetto and Beyond*, London: Virago.

Baumann, Gerd (1999) *The Multicultural Riddle: Rethinking National, Ethnic and Religious Identities*, London: Routledge.

Beck, Ulrich (1992) *Risk Society: Towards a New Modernity*, London: Sage.

Beilharz, Peter (2000) *Zygmunt Bauman: Dialectic of Modernity*, London: Sage.

Beilharz, Peter (ed.) (2001) *The Bauman Reader*, Oxford: Blackwell.

Bloch, Ernst (1986) *The Principle of Hope*, trans. Neville Plaice, Stephen Plaice and Paul Knight, 3 vols, Oxford: Blackwell.

Boltanski, Luc (1999) *Distant Suffering: Morality, Media and Politics*, trans. Graham Burchell, Cambridge: Cambridge University Press; originally published in France in 1993 as *La Souffrance à distance*.

Borges, Jorge Luis (1970) *Labyrinths: Selected Stories and Other Writings*, trans. Donald A. Yates and James E. Irby, Harmondsworth: Penguin.

Bourdieu, Pierre et al. (1999) *The Weight of the World: Social Suffering in Contemporary Society*, trans. Priscilla Parkhurst Ferguson, Susan Emmanuel, Joe Johnson and Shoggi T. Waryn, Cambridge: Polity.

Canetti, Elias (1973) *Crowds and Power*, trans. Carol Stewart, Harmondsworth: Penguin.

Castoriadis, Cornelius (1987) *The Imaginary Institution of Society*, trans. Kathleen Blamey, Cambridge: Polity.

Cohn, Norman (1967) *Warrant for Genocide*, London: Eyre and Spottiswoode.

Crozier, Michel (1964) *The Bureaucratic Phenomenon*, Chicago: University of Chicago Press.

Douglas, Mary (1966) *Purity and Danger: An Analysis of the Concepts of Pollution and Taboo*, London: Routledge and Kegan Paul.

Drucker, Peter (1989) *The New Realities*, London: Heinemann.

Ehrenberg, Alain (1998) 'L'Age de l'héroïsme: Sport, entreprise et esprit de conquête dans la France contemporaine', *Cahiers Internationaux de Sociologie*, vol. 35, pp. 197–224.

Elias, Norbert (1987) *The Society of Individuals*, ed. Michael Schroter, trans. Edmund Jephcott, Oxford: Blackwell.

Fromm, Erich (1975) *The Art of Loving*, London: Unwin Books.

Fukuyama, Francis (1992) *The End of History, and The Last Man*, Harmondsworth: Penguin.

Giddens, Anthony (1991) *Modernity and Self-identity: Self and Society in the Late Modern Age*, Cambridge: Polity.

Giddens, Anthony (1992) *The Transformation of Intimacy: Sexuality, Love and Eroticism in Modern Societies*, Cambridge: Polity.

Gillespie, Michael Allen (1995) *Nihilism before Nietzsche*, Chicago: University of Chicago Press.

Gramsci, Antonio (1971) *Selections from the Prison Notebooks*, ed. and trans. Quintin Hoare and Geoffrey Nowell Smith, London: Lawrence and Wishart.

Jonas, Hans (1984) *The Imperative of Responsibility: In Search of an Ethics for the Technological Age*, trans. H. Jonas and D. Herr, Chicago: University of Chicago Press.

Kolakowski, Leszek (1969) *Marxism and Beyond: On Historical Understanding and Individual Responsibility*, trans. Jane Zielonko Peel, London: Pall Mall Press.

Kolakowski, Leszek (1978) *Main Currents of Marxism*, vol. 3: *The Breakdown*, trans. P.S. Falla, Oxford: Clarendon Press.

Kolakowski, Leszek (1999) *Freedom, Fame, Lying and Betrayal: Essays on Everyday Life*, trans. Agnieszka Kolakowska, Harmondsworth: Penguin.

Kuhn, Thomas (1970) *The Structure of Scientific Revolutions*, 2nd edn, Chicago: University of Chicago Press.

Levinas, Emmanuel (1969) *Totality and Infinity: An Essay on Exteriority*, trans. Alphonso Lingis, Pittsburgh: Duquesne University Press.

Levinas, Emmanuel (1981) *Otherwise than Being, or Beyond Essence*, trans. Alphonso Lingis, The Hague: Martinus Nijhoff.

Marcuse, Herbert (1964) *One Dimensional Man: The Ideology of Industrial Society*, London: Routledge and Kegan Paul.

Mills, C. Wright (1959) *The Sociological Imagination*, New York: Oxford University Press.

Moore, Barrington (1978) *Injustice: The Social Bases of Obedience and Revolt*, London: Macmillan.

Peyrefitte, Alain (1998) *Du 'Miracle' en economie. Leçons au Collège de France*, Paris: Odile Jacob.

Riesman, David (1961) *The Lonely Crowd: A Study of the Changing American Character*, with Nathan Glazer and Reuel Denny, New Haven: Yale University Press.

Rorty, Richard (1991) *Objectivity, Relativism and Truth*, Cambridge: Cambridge University Press.

Schütz, Alfred (1967) *Studies in Social Theory*, vols 1 and 2, The Hague: Martinus Nijhoff.

Seabrook, Jeremy (1988) *The Race for Riches: The Human Costs of Wealth*, Basingstoke: Marshall Pickering.

Sennett, Richard (1986) *The Fall of Public Man*, London: Faber.

Sennett, Richard and Cobb, Jonathan (1972) *The Hidden Injuries of Class*, New York: Knopf.

Smith, Dennis (1999) *Zygmunt Bauman: Prophet of Postmodernity*, Cambridge: Polity.

Steiner, George (1971) *In Bluebeard's Castle: Some Notes towards the Redefinition of Culture*, London: Faber.

Steiner, George (1972) *Extra-Territorial: Papers on Literature and the Language Revolution*, London: Faber.

Tec, Nechama (1986) *When Light Pierced the Darkness*, Oxford: Oxford University Press.